Walking in the Mountains: A Woman's Guide

Walking in the Mountains

A Woman's Guide

Edith Rogovin Frankel

THE DERRYDALE PRESS
Lanham and New York

THE DERRYDALE PRESS

Published in the United States of America
by The Derrydale Press
A Member of the Rowman & Littlefield Publishing Group
4501 Forbes Boulevard, Suite 200, Lanham, Maryland 20706

Distributed by NATIONAL BOOK NETWORK, INC.

Copyright © 2003 by Edith Rogovin Frankel
First Derrydale Printing 2003

Library of Congress Control Number: 2003105131
ISBN: 1-58667-101-4 (pbk. : alk. paper)

∞™ The paper used in this publication meets the minimum requirements
of American National Standard for Information Sciences—Permanence of
Paper for Printed Library Materials, ANSI/NISO Z39.48-1992.
Manufactured in the United States of America.

For Jonny, with love

Contents

A Word of Thanks

While the concept, the writing and the walking were my own, I am grateful to a number of people for making this book what it is.

Dr. Chaya Rabnett was the source for most of the medical background and advice in this book. Chaya was intrigued by the medical aspects of various chapters and generously gave help, not only from textbooks, but from her long personal experience as a hiker as well.

I'd like to thank Tammy Soffer of Soffer Mapping, Jerusalem, whose fine map is the working model in Chapter 4. We worked together to provide a map that would enable a maximum amount of advice on map-reading, with a minimum of confusion. (Our map is based on one called "Mount Washington and the heart of the Presidential Range New Hampshire," 3rd edition, 1989, Scale 1:20,000, published by the Appalachian Mountain Club, Boston, Massachusetts.) Professor Nachman Shulman, who taught for many years in the Geology Department of the Hebrew University of Jerusalem until his retirement, was kind enough to chat with me on the fascinating history of the formation of mountains and to check my facts.

A special note of thanks to our friend Stephen Rau, an avid mountain walker who supplied me with information and a fine story.

I want to express my special appreciation to Syrell Rogovin Leahy who, besides being a great sister, has always been an example to me for creativity, energy, and resilience.

Besides members of my own immediate family, three people went over portions of the book. My friend Jezra Kaye was in at the very beginning and helped me to find the tone and style to carry the book through. Her incisive comments after a careful reading of some of the earliest writing did much to put me on the right track. I hope that she and her husband and daughter, Jerome and Larika Harris, will soon set out on their first foray into the mountains as they've promised. My agent, Phyllis Westberg, went beyond what might be the usual role of an agent, reading over the entire manuscript as the chapters rolled out and offering advice to tighten up and improve the finished product. And my dear friend Malka Jagendorf read through the whole text at the very end, pen in hand, helping with the finishing touches. This book would not have been the same without all of their devoted work.

Thanks also go to the Zermatt Tourism Office, which patiently supplied me with details on Zermatt life and tourism. Of all the various people I have run into during a lifetime of walking in the mountains, I'll single out the management and staff of Mountain Travel in Kathmandu and Delhi. The extraordinarily dedicated sardars, sherpas, and cooks (not to speak of the hard-working porters) provided us with healthy, safe treks, even during the most difficult, occasionally appalling, conditions. Though you might not be able to carry on a complicated conversation in English with many of them, they were men with whom you could entrust your life.

The artistic side of the book deserves a separate mention. My friend Ron Gordon of the Oliphant Press in New York and his colleague Aaron Tilford, provided the "look" of this book. With great patience they worked out a solution to various technical problems in order to come up with the graphic design, for which I thank them heartily. Two more very good friends gave me advice on the problem of illustrations and layout. Thanks to Evelyn Lauer Kraus and Stephanie Herman Adelman for the thought they gave to my project and to the spirit of fun with which they did it.

And now to the story of the drawings. The artist who produced the fine black and white pictures in the text is a Chinese woman whom I met by chance in Central Park. She was one of the countless park artists in New York making a modest living producing charcoal portraits of occasional customers. There was something in her drawings that made me feel that she would be the right person to do my illustrations and I approached her with a request that she reproduce one of my hiking boots. She did it admirably and after that Qun Luo (she reversed her first and last names according to English style) and I would meet in the park where I'd give her something to draw or she would present me with a finished drawing. We could hardly communicate—she knows no English and I no Chinese—but we managed with a date book, sketches and gestures. Once I brought along a Chinese-speaking friend and discovered that the woman I was dealing with had been an art professor in China. Small wonder! I would wait for her at an appointed place and she would suddenly emerge from a crowd, into which she would later disappear. I have no idea where she came from or where she went. She didn't turn up for our last meeting. I came looking for her in Central Park at other times, but never found her again. December weather in New York cut down on visits to the park, including those of the street artists. I am extraordinarily grateful to Qun Luo for her exceptional drawings and hope that sometime soon I'll again see her appearing from a crowd in Central Park and will be able to thank her in person.

It was Sandrine Larrivé-Bass who generously took time out of a busy schedule to be my Chinese–English interpreter. Thanks to his good-natured dealing with a writer's qualms, Stephen Driver, my editor, has been a pleasure to work with.

My family deserves a quantity of thanks and appreciation which would be impossible to express fully. Without them—husband, daughters, sons-in-law, and grandchildren Ariel, Eviatar, Dora and Daniel—hiking in the mountains wouldn't be as much fun. Leora and Rachel also both looked over specific chapters. Their husbands Yossi and Jonathan added advice and comments. And my husband Jonathan, who got me into all this to begin with, was part of the book from start to finish, looking over every page and walking every mile of every hike year in, year out. They and the mountains were the best part of the enterprise.

Introducing the Mountains

Chapter 1

The first present my husband bought me after our wedding was a pair of hiking boots. It was on our honeymoon. I was an American in my early twenties. We had just arrived in London, his hometown. He looked over the shoes that I had lined up in the closet of our London hotel room. "I don't understand," he said in dismay. "You *knew* we were going to the Lake District. You've only got high heels and a pair of Keds here. How do you expect to do any walking?" I frankly hadn't realized that the Lake District—an area in the north of England which boasts many beautiful lakes—was also the location of England's highest range of mountains. I had somehow pictured a few romantic days of pleasant rambles around some of the lakes. The idea of walking up through some very rugged terrain had not occurred to me. The idea that I needed special shoes for this came as a rude shock. Not wanting to get into an argument just days after we had pledged our undying love, I decided to accept the need for better footwear. Before I'd even gotten over my jet lag we went off to get a pair of "proper walking boots."

The shop that we went to has unfortunately disappeared from the face of the earth. It was part of Olde England. On a quiet street not far from Marble Arch in the middle of London we located the brownstone house with a door that had a discreet nameplate: Lawrie's. Upon our knocking, someone opened the door and led us into the interior of the building that housed the finest equippers of mountain expeditions in England, and perhaps in the world. In what must have once been a living room, we were immediately taken up by one of the shop's expert salespeople, a middle aged woman who knew everything there is to know about boots, feet, and mountains. My husband explained that, as I was a novice, he wanted a sturdy pair of boots for me, but in a soft leather that would be pliable when I took a step.

She brought out what were surely the clumsiest pair of shoes I'd ever seen. The leather was double and padded inside; the laces crisscrossed up the front; the soles were an inch thick and heavy. When I tried them on for size, I could hardly lift my feet from step to step. How was I going to walk up mountains if I couldn't even make my way across the carpet?

Never in my life had I spent so much time making sure that shoes were comfortable. The saleswoman and my husband insisted that I walk back and forth, testing for any feeling of rubbing or discomfort. "If they don't feel absolutely perfect now, then don't take them," she said. "You can't count on 'wearing them in' because once you're on the path it's too late." So I spent at least an hour making sure that these were the perfect boots for me. But it took some time before I got used to the idea of something heavy on my feet. (I later discovered that my boots were actually light compared to the ones that more experienced walkers and climbers were wearing.)

This was only the beginning, but a major first step. Those boots were going to take me up into some of the most beautiful mountains in England that week and, over the coming springs and summers, on to the White Mountains in New Hampshire, Mount Sinai, and the Swiss Alps. I had them for many, many years. In the course of that time I came to feel that those boots were one of the best things that had ever happened to me.

Mountains had always been a part of my husband's life: his family was European and regularly spent a few weeks in the Swiss Alps during the summer. My own background was far different. An American, I had never seen Europe until I was eighteen and had almost never spent time in the mountains, except for driving through the Catskills on the way to New York City from Buffalo. I always considered myself a city person. I still love cities, love to walk their streets, take in all the stores, markets, museums, the whole life of whatever city I am visiting. Being out-of-doors meant sitting in the garden behind our house. I envisioned myself as a woman who loved nature and would be happiest curled up on a sofa in front of a toasty fireplace.

So this was a real culture clash, and the way I handled it would determine how my husband and I would spend our vacations. He was very happy to travel to cities with me, but needed the mountain vacations as well. I realized that I would either join him in this or we would end up spending important vacation time apart, which I felt would be a mistake. I'd seen other couples we knew going separate ways for their vacations: he loved to ski and she couldn't stand it; she adored the beach and he found it boring. I didn't want this to happen to us.

So not only did we start taking vacations in the mountains together, but it eventually became a family thing. To be frank, I had wistfully imagined having a couple of little boys, who as they grew up would take over and keep their father company on the big climbs, leaving me to stroll happily around the village, awaiting their return. But I ended up, instead, with two girls. They turned out to be super walkers and by the time they were old enough, I found that I was enjoying the mountains too much to sit back and let them have all the fun.

This is a book about walking in the mountains. It is actually about you in the mountains, not as a bystander, not as an observer breezing by in the car. The only way to feel the real beauty of the mountains—and to gain the enormous power that they transmit—is to walk them, step by step.

Mountains provide a pastime, a splendid vacation activity. They offer aesthetic joy to the beholder and peace of mind to those who walk their paths. Beyond this, the mountain walker reaps great benefits of a different nature: the skills acquired by hikers develop physical strengths and build character.

Starting out, I had to learn how to develop my abilities. It was a slow process. I had to learn the technique of walking uphill, how to breathe, how to conserve my energy. At times it was hard, but it has given me a great source of strength. Through our vacations in the mountains I have learned to rely on stamina. I have discovered the enormous reservoir that I have in me, not only the physical strength to endure the difficulties of uphill walking in all weather, but the mental strength to organize, persevere, meet challenges. It has made me a stronger person and ultimately a more successful one.

This is what I want to share with you, this combination of factors that make a knowledge of the mountains and the ability to navigate in them so rewarding.

In the course of reading this book you'll discover the many wonderful aspects of mountain walking. You'll see not just the beauty of the

INTRODUCING THE MOUNTAINS

mountains but what they can do for you. You'll also learn how to be a mountain walker, where to go, how to conserve your strength, how to plan big walks or backpack from place to place, how to read a contour map, what's a must to carry on your back. The actual work is up to you; this book aims to lighten the load and help you to enjoy the experience to the fullest.

The Mystique of the Mountains

A few years ago, my daughter Leora and I were in Kyongju, in the southern part of South Korea. A romantic and beautiful city, Kyongju is a popular honeymoon destination for Korean couples. On our second to last day there, our hotel concierge asked if we had visited the Sokkuram Grotto, high up in the mountains several miles outside the town. He urged us to go the very next day, advising us to take a taxi early in the morning so as to get there in time to see the sunrise from the top. The concierge was so insistent that we decided, despite our natural inclination to sleep another few hours, that we would do as he suggested. The taxi arrived promptly at five the next morning and we drove up a long, winding road in the chilly dark for about half an hour until we reached the footpath. A few other hardy souls were already ahead of us. The sky became lighter as we walked, but the sun had not yet appeared. When we finally reached our destination, we found a grotto. Inside it was a Sakyamuni Buddha, made of granite, many times life size, and carved twelve hundred years ago. In its simplicity and perfection, seated serenely, cross-legged, looking out over a vista of mountains toward the East Sea, it is one of the greatest Buddhist sculptures of all time. As we took in the sight, the rays of the rising sun touched the horizon that we and the Buddha were watching and the world slowly lit up with a pure, glowing luminescence.

The mountains have a mystique. Going up a Korean mountain at sunrise to see a Buddha is one way of feeling it. But the mystique is there even without the sunrise. You feel it whenever you are among the peaks, whether walking out in the American West or in the Himalayas, whether there is a magnificent sunset or clouds have set in. It is that magic that I'd like to talk about in this chapter.

Over the years I have found that mountains are a never-ending source of magnetism. No two mountain experiences are alike; no two mountains are ever the same. They have attracted walkers, climbers, writers, artists, daredevils, and pilgrims over the millennia. Coming to the mountains after a long time is like coming home. The views, the air, the feeling of exhilaration when you set out on a new path for the first morning impart a new yet familiar sense of welcome.

Most of us grew up with romantic images of mountains. From the movie *The Sound of Music* to Johanna Spyri's *Heidi*, it was hard to think of the Alps without a sense of the romance and beauty. Did they arouse pastoral visions of goats and lambs frolicking in bright sunshine or a scene of romantic love blooming against a backdrop of snow-capped peaks? As you get older, other images join the childhood ones—ski resorts, glaciers, volcanoes, rock climbers, exotic Tibetan monasteries, lush jungles. One of these images—and probably more than one—will draw you into the mountains.

Mountains as a Life-Giving Force

To walk in the mountains is to feel invigorated. It may sound contradictory that expending energy to climb up a steep path for hours and head for bed earlier than usual for a well deserved rest would make you feel more alive. But that's just what it does. The mountain air and the unusual exertion, although you may have to catch your breath and soothe an aching muscle later, will leave you glowing with a sense of well-being and health.

It is not surprising that the ancient Chinese considered mountains to be the source of vital energies. They saw them as living organisms from which qi, or cloud vapor, emanated, dispersing the life force. You have only to walk deep into the mountains to understand how the Chinese came to this conclusion and maintained their belief for thousands of years.

Long before knowing of this Chinese image of mountains as life-giving, I felt it through my own observation. There you are up on a high slope. A stream rushes by, down toward a river below. Looking into the valley you see green fields, farms, and wild orchards, all fed by the stream flowing off the mountain. Walking in the mountains, you are part of this vitality and renewal.

In the Rockies or the Alps or any other great range, your sense of proportion is revised. Artists put this thought into images in classic Chinese scroll paintings. Those artists shared this same experience: in the paintings the mountains appear gigantic, towering over a miniature scene with a cluster of trees, a tiny bridge, and a figure or two, lost in the enormity of nature.

The life-giving force finds a different expression in Korea. In the picturesque mountains there, where you really feel that you're walking into the scene of the classical paintings—the little bridge joining two mountains over a deep chasm, the isolated mountain retreat—ancient shaman beliefs handed down from the pre-Buddhist era, still have a place in modern Korean culture.

Walk into a Buddhist temple and you are likely to find a scroll painting of the shamanist Mountain Spirit, a benign, elderly man with a white beard, sitting under a pine tree not far from a waterfall. This Mountain Spirit is held in special respect by women: he is a spirit of fertility. Women who want a baby turn to him, leaving an offering by his picture in the temple. Even when their own fertility is over, older women put coins in the box of the Mountain Spirit in the hope of longevity and prosperity. I have always felt that he epitomizes the special connection between women and mountains.

Holy Mountains

What is a holy mountain? Different peoples have different concepts of this, but I often see mountains as nature's cathedrals, rising toward the heavens, breathtaking in their majesty. Long before Columbus brought the Western Hemisphere into the European sphere, the indigenous peoples here worshipped mountains. If you look at some of the dizzying peaks in South America, you can see how awe-inspiring they were—and still are. Other mountains, like those in the American Southwest, are not as high, but were the center of ritual for the local tribes of Native Americans. Height alone is not a source of holiness. If you visit Arizona, New Mexico, or Utah, you'll feel the spirit of the mountains. There's a unique combination of sunlit peaks and stark desert below.

On a trek in Nepal, I once followed the route of pilgrims in the Himalayas for days until reaching Panch Pokari at fourteen thousand feet, where five lakes holy to Hindus glaze the surface. There they lay on a silent plateau, above the treeline, the ground covered with hoarfrost. For me they were an anticlimax. The route up had been so beautiful and the scenery so varied that getting to the top where a mist prevented us from seeing the view was almost disappointing. But the local people with

> *"What need has he of clocks who knows*
> *When highest peaks are gilt and rose*
> *Day has begun?"*
>
> —*Mary Hunter Austin*

> *"And the Lord said unto Moses, 'Come up to me into the mount, and be there: and I will give thee tables of stone, and a law, and commandments which I have written; that thou mayest teach them.' . . . And Moses went up into the mount and a cloud covered the mount. And the glory of the Lord abode upon Mount Sinai."*
>
> —*Exodus 24:12, 15–16*

us carefully circled every lake in the cold and were satisfied that they had made it to the holy spot. The next morning the sky was clear and we managed to climb up a little higher to enjoy an unforgettable panorama. That was my epiphany.

You don't have to undergo a religious experience to appreciate the special significance of being on a holy mountain. The Bible refers to Mount Sinai as the place where Moses received the Ten Commandments. Thousands of people of all kinds—intrepid travellers, lovers of mountains, pilgrims—make their way across the desert of Egypt's Sinai Peninsula every year to climb the famous mountain and to reach out to the past. There's a fine route that can be followed, allowing you to go up one way and down another (not always possible in mountainous terrain). I once made a classic mistake on Mount Sinai: I blithely followed the more clearly marked path instead of making absolutely sure that I was taking the correct way down. The result was a lengthy diversion in the wrong direction, eventually running into twilight while we were still up high, something you never want to do. In the following hours, picking my way down in the dark with a group of friends behind me, I recalled that Moses was said to have spent forty days on Mount Sinai, and hoped that it wouldn't happen to us. None of us, though, will ever forget that mountainous desert sky studded with stars of startling brightness.

Annapurna is another name for the goddess Parvati, the wife of the Hindu god, Shiva, the Moon god of the mountains. Annapurna means "filled with food." She is the Mountain goddess and it is no wonder that the Annapurna mountain was named for her. It personifies plenty, because many streams descend its slopes and water the fields and pastures below. Fittingly, the first attempt by American women to scale a mountain in the 26,000-foot category was an expedition up Annapurna I, in 1978. Two of the women succeeded in reaching the peak.

In the Himalayas some mountains are considered holy because they are the homes of gods. One of these holy mountains is Machapuchare in the Annapurna range in Nepal. A magnificent peak nearly 23,000 feet high, Machapuchare is an extraordinarily difficult mountain to climb and it is possible

THE MYSTIQUE OF THE MOUNTAINS

that no one will ever do it. In the 1950s an expedition set out to scale it, but had to turn back just before reaching the summit. Since then, the Nepali government has declared it a sacred mountain which is off limits to climbers altogether. On a trek in the Annapurna region last year, I had a view of Machapuchare almost every day from different angles, towering regally, even among giants. The knowledge that it is the home of a Hindu god and is forbidden to climbers adds to the mystery of the mountain.

Mountains as Inspiration

Once you start walking, the mountains are more than scenery, more than geological formations—perhaps because they are monumental, often remote, never heavily populated; perhaps because they are a source of natural beauty that the human hand cannot improve upon; perhaps because they appear to touch the heavens and draw us up. Whatever the source of the essential attraction of mountains, they evoke inspiration and awe.

This is why spending time in the mountains becomes both a physical and a spiritual experience. Climbing leaves me refreshed emotionally, as well as physically reinvigorated. When we first started vacationing in the mountains, I bought a little notebook, with a page for each day and I started to write up our walks. This is unusual, as I never keep a diary. It is something I only do in the mountains. On a trek, I write pages about each day, not limiting myself. There's simply so much to put down.

"What I most regret is that I kept no records of my journeyings. Never have I thought so much myself, if I may dare say it, as when I went alone and afoot."
—Jean-Jacques Rousseau

I'm sure that if I had the talent, I would take a sketchbook along. What a wonderful and relaxed way to enjoy the mountains—to carry up a pad and pastels or charcoals in your backpack, then to sit down and, while enjoying the view, to capture it in your own style. (I do take photographs; most people probably do on a vacation of this kind. But mountain photography is not so simple. It takes special technique to achieve a balance between foreground and distant peaks, to replicate on film the grandeur of the mountain scenery that you see before you in person.)

There's nothing original in finding inspiration in mountains. Think of Cezanne and his series of paintings of Mont Sainte Victoire from every conceivable angle and at different times of the day. Think of Bierstadt's glowing paintings of the Rockies. Think of Renaissance artists who incorporated views of soaring mountains as the background in their religious paintings, emphasizing the spiritual nature of their subject.

Writers, too, have been inspired by mountains. Thomas Mann's *Magic Mountain* takes place in Davos, in the Swiss Alps. John Masters' gripping novel, *High, High the Mountain Peak* has mountaineering as a central theme.

Some poets are especially connected with mountains, whether it is Robert Frost describing his own beloved New England scenery or William Wordsworth, who chose to live his life in the mountainous country of the English Lake District. Wordsworth wandered by foot all over the mountains of Cumberland, using the natural world around him as a source of inspiration for much of his poetry.

Volcanoes

Any discussion of mystique has to include the mountain that contains death and destruction within it. There is a fascination with a mountain that has a hot core and occasionally belches smoke and molten lava. I remember going to the top of Vesuvius many years ago, approaching the edge of the crater and cautiously reaching out a hand to feel the heat coming out of the center. It is a frightening and thrilling experience. Descending the

There are 540 volcanoes in the world that are still active. Three quarters of them are in the areas of the Pacific rim—along the west coast of North and South America, running from Alaska down to Chile, and in Asia from Siberia down to New Guinea and New Zealand.

mountain to visit Pompeii or Herculaneum, two Roman cities that were destroyed by an eruption of Mount Vesuvius over two thousand years ago, you feel the power of the angry force within the volcano.

Some people make a point of climbing volcanoes: there are a host of them in Latin America with exotic names out of the pre-Columbian world like Popocatépetl, Iztaccihuatl, Chimborazo. Ascending any of these volcanoes involves a major climb, but you can hike in the lower mountains in the area and enjoy the view of the great peaks. In the American state of Washington, Mount Rainier, which hasn't erupted in over a century, is the highest mountain in the Cascade range. This volcano of almost fourteen and a half thousand feet is a magnet for intrepid climbers.

The Historic Attraction

People often try to combine their vacations with a glimpse of history: following Civil War battles, visiting the beaches of Normandy, checking out Bunker Hill and Breed's Hill in Boston. You can do this on a mountain vacation too.

One day we were passing through the French town of Chambery, on our way to a walking vacation in the French Alps, when my husband and I came across a statue of an elephant. It seemed bizarre to see it in a part of Europe that is more likely to host deer and rabbits as its predominant wildlife. And then we remembered Hannibal. The elephant commemorated Carthage's famous attack on Rome over two thousand years ago, when Hannibal's troops, replete with elephants, made an epic crossing of the Alps over the pass at Mont Genevre to invade Italy from the north. It boggles the mind to imagine those massive animals making their way over the Alps and, while they succeeded, the feat has never been duplicated. After a day's walk in the area, a history buff might well want to read from Livy's account of this, one of the most famous invasions in the ancient world.

I always enjoy hiking around Bear Mountain State Park, not far from New York City. Some of the trails there follow the original routes taken by hostile armies during the Revolutionary War. They're well marked and walking there brings you closer to the historic events in the Hudson River valley over two hundred years ago.

The Sheer Danger of Mountains

Very often, when you're walking in the mountains, there's a view of higher peaks in the vicinity, snow-capped, covered with glaciers. Those views make your walks all the more exciting, although there's little chance that you'll ever climb the really tough ones yourself. But it's these very mountains and the element of danger they hold that attracts some people. The challenge of climbing the very hardest peaks—Mount Everest, K-1, the north wall of the Eiger—is what draws a small number of men and women to take enormous risks.

I myself have never wanted to climb the great mountains; I am not attracted by a physical challenge that includes laboring up a mountain face when there is too little oxygen or risk of frostbite. But I do find that these peaks have an aura of beauty and danger that fascinates me. And when you're walking in the mountains, even if you never use a rope or pitons, you can vicariously understand what it means to climb the highest peaks, just as knowing how to play a musical instrument, however modestly, helps to appreciate the genius of a musician you hear at a concert. You often find that you are caught up in the challenge and romance of climbing efforts.

Staying at the Swiss resort of Grindelwald, in the Bernese Oberland, I have frequently used the telescope set up on the main street of the village to watch the progress of what looks like three spiders making their way across the north face of the Eiger. The atmosphere in villages overshadowed by famous peaks—the Eiger, the Matterhorn, the high Himalayas—is often suffused with the mystique of the great climbs.

Mountains that are Lush and Peaceful

Now that I've talked about the exotic attributes of mountains, I'll turn to a less dramatic aspect, but one which has its own fascination for me.

After all the sheer height and magnificence, after the snow and glaciers, the barren rocky towers, I love to turn to the softer nature also to be found in many mountain regions—the thickly wooded slopes, the high pastures covered with flowers in the spring, the spectacular colors in the fall.

There are mountains that are the grazing grounds for sheep, goats, and cows. The clink of the cowbells on a sunny day as you make your way up a mountainside may not be captured in your photo album but forever resounds in your memory.

In some areas, instead of pastureland or woodland, mountains are used for agriculture, their steep sides terraced for intensive farming. In the United States and Canada, with their seemingly boundless land, there has been little need to tame mountainsides. But travel to the Italian Apennines and you will see grapevines carefully tended on their terraced slopes. Here every inch is exploited and the result is a marvelous, crazy quilt of different crops all the way up.

In the Himalayas, you can look up thousands of feet and see step upon step of bright green rice plants growing on terraced land and, above that, the darker green of millet. I have walked for whole days along the edges of terraced land in Nepal and India, balancing precariously to avoid stepping on the crop growing on the few yards of fertile soil to my left or falling off the edge to my right down to the next level of green. The view is breathtaking, but you'd better not take your eyes off the path!

Being in the mountains, any mountains, means that there are splendid views wherever you look: maybe of other mountains, maybe of valleys and lakes below. They are unlike any sight you can find elsewhere. And the panorama is enhanced by the sounds: the sound of the wind, the cowbells, the bubbling streams, the waterfalls, the crunch of the ground under your boots. The views, the sounds, and the clear fresh air add to the mystique that you feel in the mountains, an incomparable freshness and beauty.

> *"They climbed together, at evening, up the high slope, to see the sun set. In the finely breathing, keen wind they stood and watched the yellow sun skink in crimson and disappear. Then in the east the peaks and ridges glowed with living rose, incandescent like immortal flowers against a brown-purple sky, a miracle, whilst down below the world was a bluish shadow, and above, like an annunciation, hovered a rosy transport in mid air. . . . To her it was so beautiful, it was a delirium, she wanted to gather the glowing, eternal peaks to her breast."*
> —*Women in Love*, D. H. Lawrence

Starting Out

Whether it is the danger, the pristine views, the lush foliage and quiet paths, the snow and ice, the mountains draw you to them. To enter that world, you need good strong boots, a backpack, and the energy to seek out that special magic. Let's get started!

Getting Fit for Your Adventure

Chapter 3

Fit for Walking

When he was sixteen years old, my husband set out to climb the Matterhorn. It is the most famous of the many mountains over 13,000 feet that surround the tiny Swiss village of Zermatt. The rule for that mountain is one guide to one person on the rope. It is also the rule that if you set out on the climb, you have to pay the guide, even if you don't manage to complete it. A short time after they began their ascent, it started to snow and they had to turn back. The fee was paid and my husband was disappointed.

His next attempt was thirty years later during a family vacation. We'd spent a week getting into good condition, hiking up and down mountains and backpacking. It took him ten hours to get to the top of the Matterhorn and return to the Hörnli Hut where the climb had begun. On the mountain with him that day were two other climbers and their Swiss guides. Hans, a German, was in his fifties and quite a bit older than my husband, but he managed to do the climb in the shortest time and with the least effort.

The next night we went out to a *stübli* for a drink with Hans and his wife. My husband was struck by Hans' ability and stamina and Hans explained that he ran a few miles a day regularly. That was how he had built up his capacity to complete a rigorous climb like the Matterhorn. It was after this that my husband decided to include walking and jogging as part of his weekday schedule, about three-quarters of an hour before breakfast. As he is very slow to wake up in the morning, this is also a useful way for him to become alert earlier.

Though I'm not talking about rock climbing, but about walking in the mountains, the lesson is just as clear. While you don't have to be a fanatic about exercise, a regular dose will stand you in good stead, not only for the mountains but for your daily life.

Deciding on Your Fitness Needs

Luckily, there is an endless source of ranges to choose from, near and far, when you are thinking ahead to your vacation. The last few chapters in this book will give you plenty of food for thought on the question of "where"? The next question is: do I have to work on my fitness before heading for the mountains?

The answer actually depends on two factors: *your state of fitness and the level of difficulty of the walking you plan to do*. Only after you consider both of these factors will you know how much you'll have to prepare yourself in advance.

Your State of Fitness

Let's look at some categories of fitness and see where you belong:

1   LITTLE REGULAR EXERCISE
    You are, to put it simply, a "couch potato." At work, you sit at a desk most of the day. If someone is going down to pick up coffee, you ask him to bring you some too so that you don't have to get up. Or you get in some walking, standing, bending, whether it's making beds, teaching a class, or greeting customers. Aside from that, you're not likely to have much exercise. If there's a newspaper store at the corner, you will hop in the car to get there. *You need to know what it's like to walk. Start practicing.*

2   A NORMALLY ACTIVE WOMAN
    You're in good shape physically and weigh within a reasonable range of what's recommended. You do a fair amount of walking as part of your normal schedule and you don't tire running up a flight of stairs. You don't actually have an organized fitness routine, but you get a lot of exercise in as a matter of course. You love the idea of walking in the mountains but are not sure if you like the idea of an exercise program. If you start out slowly once you get to the mountains, you should be able to build up your stamina and walking skills while you're there. *If you don't plan to spend a lot of time in the mountains, start practicing before you leave.*

3   ROBUST, WHETHER IN YOUR TWENTIES OR FIFTIES

You're an active person, even if your job has you sitting on your fanny much of the day. You take the opportunity to get up whenever you can, whether to refill your cup or run out to pick up some lunch to bring back to eat at your desk. You do some kind of exercise a couple of times a week and on the weekend. It's not your main occupation, but you are in good shape. You can run for a bus without getting out of breath. But you'd probably like to skip taking the bus altogether and walk. *Keep up what you're doing and you'll do fine in the mountains.*

4   IN ABSOLUTELY TOP FORM

You don't have an extra pound on your body. You're firm, have good muscles. You spend a lot of time in the gym working out. You run miles, after work and on the weekend. It's not just a healthy habit: it's a way of life. You really miss it if you don't have your exercise one day. *You're ready for the whole range of mountain hikes.*

Summary

If you're in the first category, plan to do some of the exercising recommended later in this chapter, but if you are in reasonable condition (level 2), you can consider heading straight for the mountains and acclimating there. If you're in one of the last two groups (levels 3–4), go ahead and enjoy yourself (unless you've got a very hard climb planned), though it's still worth getting used to the terrain and the altitude gradually, once you are up in the hills. Remember that paths vary, so in the same resort area there are both difficult and gentle climbs. It's like skiing: you can find a simple blue run or a killer black piste in the same area, so you just have to pick the one that's best suited to your ability.

Level of Difficulty

A few years ago, a friend of mine, a self-described couch potato, started to become interested in mountain walking after looking through one of our photo albums. They're really beautiful—unbelievable pictures of mountain scenery, little villages nestled far below in the valleys, us looking incredibly relaxed and healthy against the backdrop of magnificent peaks. She started asking me whether she could do something like that and, in the course of our conversation, voiced some of the concerns and questions that you may have.

SALLY: Hey, this looks great, but I don't know if it's for me. I mean, don't you think it's too tough for someone in my lousy shape?

ME: Look, there are two things—what kind of condition you're in and how difficult the mountains are. As far as the mountains are concerned, you just do what you can cope with. You don't have to aim for the highest peak in the region. There are easy walks, or moderate ones, to start with.

SALLY: Yeah, easy. For you. What you mean by easy may not be what I mean. Are they going to have to send out a St. Bernard with some brandy for me when I collapse?

ME: Very funny. An easy walk is something that you can do, too. What I'd suggest is that you start out with a walk that'll just take a morning. That is, you'll climb about a thousand feet—that can take anything from an hour to an hour and a half—stop and have a bite to eat and a drink, and then walk back. You can usually count on the walk down as taking a third less time than the walk up. So the whole thing would be two to three hours, including your stop.

SALLY: O.K. That doesn't sound too bad, though I don't remember the last time I walked for two hours straight. Actually, isn't that exhausting?

ME: You'll have to be careful not to push yourself. Just walk at a steady pace and make sure not to get winded. It's not a race, you know.

SALLY: And you think that I can just go out and do it?

ME: Frankly, I think that you'd enjoy your vacation more if you were in a little better condition than you are now. You'll probably want to start out with some walking before you leave home. To tell you the truth, I think you'll be doing yourself a big favor anyway by getting off that couch sometimes.

Sally liked the idea of getting ready first with a little exercise and then starting with an easy program in the mountains. She eventually became very enthusiastic and also more ambitious, finally getting into exciting vacations which demanded a lot of stamina. She now has her own great photo albums to impress her friends with.

What are the levels of difficulty that you can encounter in mountain terrain? (See the last four chapters for descriptive examples.)

An *easy walk* takes you up a short distance with a gradual ascent of between one and two thousand feet on a clearly marked path. It's always a good idea to start on this kind of walk—climbing for an hour and a half to two hours—on the first day you're in the mountains, so that you can acclimate to the walking, the ascent, and the altitude.

> **PREPARATION FOR AN EASY WALK: If you're in the "little exercise" category you'll want to prepare yourself in order to make your mountain vacation more successful. Get started with a walking program before leaving home.**

A *moderate walk* involves a climb of three to four thousand feet. As it normally takes fifty minutes to an hour to ascend one thousand feet in a direct ascent, this kind of walk will take at least three or four hours to get to the high point. You'll be on the move steadily, maybe pause for a drink, but—in mountaineering tradition—probably wait until you get to the top or just beyond it to sit down and have your lunch. Then it will take another few hours to get back. So the walk will take up the better part of the day.

PREPARATION FOR A MODERATE WALK: Don't start out on your first day with a moderate climb unless you arrive in the mountains in splendid condition. You should begin with a day or two of easy climbing and then move on to the moderate level. Even so, you'll do better if you've prepared yourself with some walking or running before leaving home.

The *demanding walk* (which covers the range between moderate and strenuous) includes greater distance and a climb of up to five thousand feet in a day. That is really a serious amount of walking and you will be on the go for six to nine hours. You'll need more stamina for this. There are big payoffs, of course, when you do a climb like this: new and spectacular views, stretching yourself more, sitting up on top of a peak and looking down at the clouds and the birds flying below.

PREPARATION FOR A DEMANDING WALK: You're probably in pretty good shape to begin with if you're planning this kind of climb. But you'll want to prepare with a few days' easy and moderate walking in the mountains where you're vacationing before you're ready to tackle this level of difficulty. It certainly pays to have paved the way with an exercise routine at home.

A *strenuous walk* requires more stamina and effort, involves a steep gradient, thousands of feet of up and down, high altitude walking, possibly snow or glacier crossings, sometimes the use of crampons and many hours of effort. Strenuous walking may also mean backpacking—walking from place to place with your backpack carrying everything you'll need for a few days—or trekking, which is an extended form of backpacking popular in many mountainous regions, such as the Sierra Nevadas or the Himalayas. Here a large part of the effort, besides the actual climbing, is in the length of time you're on the trail.

PREPARATION FOR STRENUOUS WALKING: For this you must build up your stamina to its maximum. Unless you are in superb physical shape, you should engage in a serious fitness program before leaving home.

I've outlined the major differences between the levels of walking you may encounter, but remember that there are always variables such as terrain and weather that will affect the difficulty of a walk beyond the simple question of how high and how far. Height here has two meanings: how many feet you ascend in a given day or how far above sea level you are walking. Altitude plays a big part. The higher the altitude, the more breathless you become. When you're first at 10,000 feet, you will find that even the most ordinary physical action becomes an effort. A walk that at sea level would be categorized as moderate, is much more difficult if you start from a very high point, for example, in Aspen, Colorado. Because of this, don't plan as ambitious an itinerary for your first few days if you are starting at a high altitude. I'll be discussing altitude-related questions later.

This gives you some idea of the amount of effort you will be expending, and how that tallies with your physical condition today. Whatever your level of fitness and ambition, you'll probably find yourself trying to prepare in advance for the next level up.

WOMEN IN THE MOUNTAINS

"[In the 1880s] there was another woman on the scene—Mrs. Aubrey LeBlond. . . . She was one of the most elegant and one of the most intrepid women who ever scaled a mountain. She climbed in winter as well as in summer and was usually accompanied by her lady's maid. Victorian proprieties still had to be observed and although Mrs. LeBlond wore climbing breeches for her actual ascents she always left Zermatt clad in a skirt. The garment was removed after the last cow had been passed and was carried in the guide's rucksack. There is a story . . . that she climbed the Zinal Rothorn [a near fourteen thousand foot Alpine peak] from Zermatt and, having reached the summit, descended to Zinal. As she approached the village it was discovered that her skirt had been left on the summit. The guide was full of consternation, but in Mrs. LeBlond's view only one course could be followed. The party about turned, toiled up to the summit once more, retrieved the skirt and descended to Zermatt."
—Cicely Williams, Zermatt Saga

Just being young and physically active does not guarantee that you'll take to the hills like a mountain goat. On my first visit to the Swiss Alps, in my mid-twenties, I had an embarrassing experience. I started up the path leading out of the village. It began with an extraordinarily steep slope and I quickly found myself winded. Crawling along at a snail's pace and trying to catch my breath, I saw a little old lady striding up the steep path, walking stick in hand. In a moment she had caught up and then passed me while I, at least fifty years younger than she, struggled slowly on.

In spite of this, mountain walking *is* something that most people can do and enjoy. This book will show you how.

Mountain walking is exactly what it sounds like: walking uphill. There's none of the dramatic footage seen in documentary films of a human fly clinging to the rock face, fastened to her companions by a rope. We occasionally get roped up for a particular walk—a very steep snowy ascent to a mountain peak or crossing a glacier slashed by crevasses. But this is not a necessary or even usual feature of mountain walking.

Getting into Shape

With a small investment of time, you can build up strength and stamina very simply. It won't happen overnight, though, and I recommend that you begin your program two months before your trip. If you have to lose any weight, this is a good time to do it. There is no need to attack the problem of your fitness as a full time job or let it take over all of your free time. *How much you exercise depends on your present fitness and how ambitious your mountain plans are.* Here are some of the methods that work for me.

Walking
Do as much walking as you can. If your place of work—or the local store or your school—is within a few hundred yards or even a mile or two of your home, *don't drive, don't take a bus: walk.* Walk briskly: it's excellent aerobic exercise and you'll get there faster. Remember that the more quickly you walk, the more calories you burn, the greater the benefit.

If it doesn't make sense to walk to work, then *set aside some other time of day to get in twenty to thirty minutes of brisk walking* at least three times a week. The most convenient time may be during your lunch break. During a period of four years when I was the director of a busy office in Manhattan, I got my basic exercise a couple of times a day. I walked to work every morning across Central Park (and home again during the summer months when it remained light late enough) and I took a good walk at lunchtime, sometimes taking off time to pick up my lunch. In this way, I managed to clock in two to three miles a day, and enjoyed it.

Walk early in the morning if it suits your schedule or in the evening when the day cools down, but walk!

Make it a routine activity. Don't just take a walk when you have the time or inclination: put your walk into your schedule.

If you walk briskly, you should average between three and four miles an hour. Don't just stroll. Don't stop to look in store windows; keep moving. Even so, you'll find that walking is interesting: you'll get to know your neighborhood better. You'll see things on foot that you never noticed driving past in the car. And it's a wonderful time to do some thinking.

HINT:

To maximize your walking as exercise, carry a small backpack. It will add a little weight and approximate mountain walking needs.

Some people don't like to walk alone. Walk with a friend, your husband, your neighbor, or alone, but walk!

Running

You can get even more out of the time that you exercise if you run. Instead of burning five or six calories a minute walking, you can burn ten or twelve, depending on your speed and your weight. Other benefits of exercise, besides just calorie count, also increase with running.

Running is not for everyone, but it is a great joy for those who like it. I was never into running until I started preparing for our first trek in the Himalayas. My goal was to get into as good condition as I could as quickly as possible. I have a career; I have a family. Time is very precious to me as it is to many women who have to fulfill multiple roles in their lives. So it made sense, if I could only spare half an hour or forty minutes a day—and not even every day—to use that time as efficiently as possible. I started using a treadmill at a fitness club so that I could keep track of my speed and distance. Using the treadmill gave me the base speed and time from which I could improve.

I began by running just a quarter of a mile and then switching to a brisk walk. During the next twenty to thirty minutes I alternated running and walking. As the weeks went by, I gradually stretched the distance that I ran and also increased my walking and running speed. When I got up to running a mile or so, I decided to run around the reservoir in Central Park, which is 1.57 miles. To my amazement, though I'd never actually run that far on the treadmill, I was able to do it without taking a break.

If you live in New York, or are visiting, the experience of circling the reservoir (famous because all sorts of well-known people—such as Jackie Kennedy—have been spotted) is the recommended, at least occasionally. It's useful and fun, wherever you live, to run with the herd every once in a while. Some people will pass you; you'll eventually manage to overtake others and someone will be running at just the right speed to pace you. But however the others run, it's a special kind of social experience that's worth trying.

It may seem strange that someone who had been walking in mountains—some of them very high and demanding—for many years should not have been able to run a mile easily right off. But walking, swimming, running all involve different skills and while each contributes to fitness there is no reason to think that if you do one form of exercise well you can automatically be a good runner too.

WHERE TO RUN

In your town there may be good *running courses* that you can use. These often have markers for every half mile so that you know exactly how far you've come and can keep track of your speed. They are often especially pleasant to use because they are in parks and landscaped.

You can also run on the *track around the stadium* at your local high school or sports club. Generally the whole way round the outer edge of a football field is a quarter of a mile, or four hundred meters. This makes it easier for you to know the distance that you're running. The track is usually very comfortable underfoot. What you don't want is to run on a hard surface, like concrete or asphalt. It's not good for the knees and feet. I always stay away from roads because I don't like getting all the exhaust from cars in my face when I'm breathing deeply.

If you have a young child, you may have a problem getting away for a run: even thirty minutes is a valuable chunk of time for a mother. But there are now three-wheeled strollers designed specifically for running. The handle is extra long and at a good height to give you a comfortable grip and position while running. Babies seem to enjoy whirling along in their strollers pushed by a jogging parent.

Another good possibility for running, as I've already indicated, is a *treadmill*. The disadvantage is that it's extremely boring to run in place indoors. Running outside is really more fun.

IF YOU HAVE BLADDER OR INCONTINENCE PROBLEMS:
Impact exercise, on hard or softer surfaces, should be avoided. You should be concentrating on low-impact exercise instead.

But there are many advantages. First, you can run in any weather. Second, you have a very controlled situation so that you know precisely how fast you are running, and how far. You can fiddle around with the controls to stretch your capacity and gradually increase your speed. The main thing is to start gradually and avoid pushing forward faster than you can manage.

In any of these situations you can compete with yourself, with your past performance, and gradually develop the stamina that is so important when you're up in the mountains. You're playing a noncompetitive game, where the only "opponent" is yourself. There's a tremendous feeling of accomplishment when you see the steady improvement that comes with a consistent program of walking or running.

Walking Uphill
One of the best preparations for the mountains is actually walking uphill. If you have a hill or mountain within easy reach of your home,

you should take off an afternoon now and then and simply walk up and down it. If it's really small, do it a number of times. Walking downhill is every bit as important because you use different muscles when you go down a mountain. Often—and you will understand what I mean when you're up on the trail—it is actually easier to walk uphill than down. It is true that you expend more energy on the ascent, but you need much more control on the way down.

Use stairs instead of an elevator whenever possible. Do it at home and do it at work. Of course you may not want to walk up to the fourteenth floor in your office building. But you can at least walk up and down a flight or two.

Before we went on our first trek to the Himalayas I decided to ignore the fact that my office building had an elevator and simply walked up the stairs from the underground parking lot to my department on the fifth floor. If you do this, in a few days you'll notice that you're not out of breath and get up the stairs much more quickly.

Again, *if you're using a treadmill,* you can set it to an incline and then run or walk "uphill" on it. You can set it for different angles as well as different speeds and gradually increase your stamina. Even if you just walk up the incline for a minute or two and then flatten out the treadmill again, you can repeat this from time to time and reap real benefits. This is something that I do regularly and I have found that it is much easier for me to get acclimatized to uphill walking on the first day in the mountains than it used to be.

Step machines can also give an approximate uphill motion. Some people find them very effective. Check at your local health club—there is a wide variety of machines available now for developing specific skills and abilities. And more are appearing all the time.

MAINTAINING FITNESS
- **Walk regularly**
- **Jog**
- **Walk uphill and downhill**
- **Use the stairs**
- **Avoid the elevator**
- **Work out**
- **Eat nutritious foods**

- **Watch your weight**
- **Play, don't be a spectator**

Summing Up

My own regular routine is to walk whenever I can avoid using the car, to use the stairs instead of an elevator and to do controlled running and walking on the treadmill two or three days a week for at least half an hour at a stretch.

When I am preparing for major walking—a two-week trek, for example—I step up the program by going to the fitness room more often. My routine is not necessarily for longer, but I go at least four times a week and set the incline on the treadmill for extended periods of brisk walking. I also try to take off any excess pounds I have put on.

Whenever it's possible, I also spend time walking up and down hills in preparation for the bigger ones I'll be climbing. For a major expedition, I will also try to spend some time in the mountains before the trek in order to acclimate to the altitude and the sustained effort.

A Healthy Attitude

I must admit that when I first decided to start running, my younger daughter, Rachel, expressed real concern. The basic message was that at my age—I was over fifty—it could be very dangerous. She urged me to check with my doctor first. When I spoke to him, he said, "I'd be much more worried if you *didn't* run than if you did." So off I went.

Even if you're only planning a single mountain holiday, the exercise you do in preparation is no waste of time. Walking in the mountains is a healthy activity; so is all exercise, whether in the gym or on a track. None of this is wasted effort and you will be contributing to your own physical well-being. Recent studies show that sound health habits, a nutritious diet, and a consistent fitness program contribute not only to a longer life, but to a healthier old age.

There is convincing scientific evidence of "a significant inverse relationship between activity level and mortality rate." Scientists found that the number of deaths attributable to cardiovascular or respiratory causes decreased in proportion to the increase in the energy spent on activities including walking, stair climbing, and sports.

CHECK WITH A DOCTOR BEFORE PLANNING YOUR TRIP OR STARTING EXERCISE IF:

- **You have high blood pressure (over 140/90)**
- **You have angina or irregular heart rhythm**
- **You have asthma**
- **You are anemic**
- **You are pregnant**

Regular exercise, at least twenty minutes of real exertion three times a week, contributes to cardiovascular fitness—that is, the efficiency of the heart and lungs in extracting oxygen from the bloodstream. The better the cardiovascular fitness, the lower the pulse, another goal of working out regularly. Exercise is also a key factor in the control of obesity. Obesity is related to a higher incidence of heart problems and diabetes.

What is meant by "real exertion" in exercise? Simply put, you should work up a sweat, feel that you are pushing yourself. Technically, you should be raising your pulse during exercise. How much? There's an easy formula: Take 220 and subtract your age. Your pulse should be between 50 and 75% (closer to 75%) of that figure. So a woman of thirty would work it out in the following way:

> ### THE *NEW YORK TIMES* ON OSTEOPOROSIS
> *"The sooner preventive treatment is started, the better. The new guidelines suggest that all men and women, regardless of current bone density, consume adequate amounts of calcium and Vitamin D; get regular weight-bearing exercise like walking, jogging, stair climbing, dancing and tennis; avoid tobacco use and abuse of alcohol."*
> *(November, 1998)*

> 220 − 30 = 190
> 75% of 190 = 143.5
> **That's a pulse rate of 143 after exercise.**

(Your ordinary pulse at rest may be between 60 and 90.)

A woman of sixty would have the following formula:

> 220 − 60 = 160
> 75% of 160 = 120 pulse rate after exercise

Besides the general benefits of a regular program of exercise, there are many benefits specific to women.

BENEFITS OF EXERCISE
- Reduced premenstrual symptoms
- Decreased incidence of lower back pain
- Symptoms of lower bowel syndrome reduced
- Increased sense of well-being during menopause
- Prevention of osteoporosis
- Good muscle tone
- Cardiovascular fitness

It doesn't matter if you haven't been exercising all your life: whenever you begin, at twenty, forty or sixty, your body will benefit. *Studies now show that even when the extremely old start to exercise, they acquire muscle tone and see significant improvement in their physical well being.*

> *"Too many older people with life-long unhealthy habits assume that it is too late to change and reap benefits from quitting smoking, starting exercise, losing weight or eating a more nutritious diet. The findings [of the research of John Rowe and Robert Kahn] show otherwise. . . . Perhaps the broadest benefits to both body and mind accrue from becoming more physically active, even after eight decades on the couch."*
> —New York Times, *April 1998*

A slender neighbor of mine was horrified to discover, after a complete physical examination, that while her weight was fine, her level of fitness was catastrophic. She couldn't believe it, because she assumed that, being wonderfully slim, she was fitter than heavier people she knew. But she soon realized that taking her car back and forth to the lab where she worked every day, with no time given to exercise at all, had left her incredibly weak. She could hardly operate the stationary bicycle during her physical examination. On doctor's orders, she immediately started to take walks every evening when she came home from work. (Her husband, after his own warning from the doctor, joined her.)

We get less exercise today than people did in the first half of the century. Until several decades ago, most people were routinely engaged in more physical activity. Many occupations—and this applies to both men and women—involved far greater effort than they do today. Now we have machines to do much of our work. Whether you are cleaning a rug, beating eggs or drilling a hole in the wall, you're using less energy than men and women did before there were vacuum cleaners, electric mixers, and power drills. People are simply doing less lifting, pushing, and bending.

Many people rarely walk. "Exercise" is reduced to walking from the car park to the mall. Without thinking twice, you jump into the car to get a newspaper or milk at a store that's just a few minutes away. What this amounts to, unless you perform some kind of physically active work, strenuous or not, is that you have to find some other way to keep yourself fit.

> **PHYSICAL FITNESS IN THE MOUNTAINS:** If walking is good exercise, walking uphill is even better. It expends more energy, utilizes more muscles, speeds up your pulse, increases lung activity—it's an efficient system of promoting cardiovascular activity. Your benefits multiply, not just because of the additional effort, but also because the effort is expended over a prolonged period of time.

You're Looking Better

With all this walking, jogging, walking up stairs, you will begin to notice that, even if you haven't lost an ounce, you look better. You are firmer, you have good muscle tone. Your clothes fit you better.

My experience over many years of walking in the mountains is that by the end of the first week or ten days, my stomach is flat. What your daily exercise doesn't accomplish, a week or two in the mountains will.

Uphill walking utilizes calf muscles and thighs. It also works in the same way that an "abs" class does, so the abdominal muscles are strengthened. If you haven't used these muscles sufficiently before your visit to the mountains, you'll feel them the first night or two. But this shouldn't last for more than a few days.

When my daughter Rachel decided to go on a strenuous trek in the Himalayas recently I advised her to exercise as much as possible before going or she'd never make it all the way. She joined a health club and started using the treadmill, walking at a fast pace for half an hour at a stretch. At some point she decided that, although she never particularly cared for running she would try it: the fact that her mother did it became a kind of challenge. She found, after a couple of months, that she was easily running two miles without even feeling breathless. And what a difference in her appearance! I could hardly believe how great she looked.

MUSCLES THAT ARE USED

Uphill:

- *Hip flexors (upper thigh muscles)*
- *Hamstring muscles (back thigh)*
- *Calf muscles*

Downhill:

- *Quadriceps (front thigh)*
- *Calf muscles*

Diet

This brings me to a related subject. You don't have to be thin to be a good mountain walker. But you will find that if you carry less weight uphill it is easier. If you are thinking of losing weight anyway, you might as well do it before your vacation.

The corollary of this is that mountain walking itself will help you to keep down your weight and even to lose it. We have certainly found that a hard day's walking uphill and downhill burns so many calories that even if we eat a heartier dinner than usual, including a good dessert, we never gain weight on a mountain vacation. Even more, on the really big treks people often lose weight. Walking every day all day for a couple of weeks uses so much energy that even the best of camp chefs can't fatten you up with meals.

Walking uphill increases the number of calories that are used. Even a slow and steady climb, when done hour after hour, uses up energy. At the end of the day, if you have walked uphill and down, say, for five hours, you will have burned up at the very least 1,500 calories above and beyond what you usually use in a day. That's much more than you can work off walking along a flat road—or playing a social game of tennis or golf.

ADVANTAGES OF CONTROLLING OBESITY

- **Lower chances of diabetes**
- **Decreased chances of breast cancer**
- **Decreased chances of colon cancer**
- **Decreased likelihood of varicose veins**
- **Less chance of incontinence after childbearing years**
- **Decreased incidence of lower back pain**

The Psychology of Fitness

Many people feel better after exercise. You can work out tensions while walking or running. If you have a headache when you come into the fitness room you can lose it by the time you leave.

Besides the clear physical advantages of being fit and maintaining the right weight is the psychological factor, the clear connection between the body and the psyche. Look at the way people deal with stress. Many people unwind by walking; a good long walk can be therapeutic. An hour in the gym can leave you feeling like a new person.

This is not only a psychological phenomenon. There is a physical explanation for it. During exercise, chemicals called endorphins are released and they produce a sense of well-being. They do even more than that. They also reduce pain perception so that people with chronic pain syndrome feel better while they are exercising and even beyond: endorphins produce an extended effect.

Exercise provides clear benefits on the routine level. During a mountain vacation you will find that the physical and mental advantages reaped by days of intensive exercise grow exponentially. I find that even a week in the hills is enough to revive and exhilarate me. The combination of all that walking in the fresh air, enjoying the mountainous scenery, talking and, ultimately, being quiet with my own thoughts is truly the best cure for all the tensions, tiredness, and concerns of ordinary life.

And nowadays I'm the one who strides up the path past a beginning climber who's catching her breath. I hope that I'll still be doing it in my eighties.

Map Reading and Other Useful Skills

Although you probably won't need a map on some of your early walks, you should always take one with you. Assuming that you select a clear path and that it is well-marked, none of the main aids—maps, compass, altimeter—is necessary. Don't feel that you can't take a hike on a nearby mountain without being a trained navigator. Nevertheless, it's good practice to have a map and to get into the habit of checking it because it will be your best friend during your walking career.

> *"Journey over all the universe in a map, without the expense and fatigue of traveling, without suffering the inconveniences of heat, cold, hunger, and thirst."*
> —*Miguel de Cervantes*

Why Do You Need a Map?

For both planning before you hit the path and while you're on it:

- A map informs you how far you have gone and how much further you have to walk to get to your destination.
- It indicates not only distance but altitude—how much climbing you will have to do.
- A good map, carefully read, should give you a good idea of how difficult or easy the path is and helps you plan your day's walking.
- Use it to figure out the best place to stop and have lunch.
- A map can help you decide which of two alternative paths to the same place you should choose.
- A map shows you what you can expect to see along the way—a stream to be crossed, a nearby farm, a lake, a hostel, or hotel.
- It will also indicate the landscape of the area and inform you of the kind of terrain you will be crossing—a marsh, a forest, rock—all these are shown on a good topographical map.

- Using your map you will be able to identify the neighboring mountains and put a name on them.
- In general, the map will indicate most points of interest that you're near and give their names.
- Most important, a map should keep you from being lost. If all else fails—no signposts, the path fades out, no cairns, trail markers disappear — it is with a map (and a compass) that you can find your way.

Finding a Map

If you are walking in a state park or a national park, you can usually get a map showing the various paths in the area from the local park rangers office. They will also be able to advise you on the condition and difficulty of particular trails. It's a good idea to consult someone in a park office if you can—has a path been washed out? Is the route I'm considering good for an average walker? Is there still snow higher up on the path? (Once, in Arizona, I was advised by a park ranger that there was a broad swath of snow and ice on the path we planned to use. Luckily, there was a nearby shop where we could rent crampons for our shoes and that made all the difference to us: we were able to handle a walk that would have been too slippery otherwise.)

If you are planning a walk in an area where a rangers office of this type is not at hand, local sports stores, book shops, or a tourist information office will have hiking maps that you can take or buy.

What you're looking for is a topographical map of the area, that is, a map that presents a full picture of the terrain down to minute details. This should include a rendering of the relief so that you can tell—through the coloring, shading and contour lines—what the lay of the land is, where there are mountains and valleys. Paths, roads, and other features are also on such a map.

Let's Look at a Map

It is amazing what a world of information is contained on a single sheet of paper. Sit down and take a careful look at a map. It is truly a picture of a region that provides more detail than you could get in pages of writing.

Most maps that hikers use are topographical maps produced by national surveys—for instance, the U.S. Geological Survey maps of

America or the British Ordnance Survey maps. Some of them were produced a long time ago and you will occasionally notice that the map differs slightly from the situation on the ground. Not only may some structure be missing or some other building appear, but it is even possible that a stream bed has changed since the map was created. The date that the map was made should appear somewhere on the map, though however old, it may be the best available for your purposes.

Before anything else, look at the legend. Without this, the map will not be able to tell its full story. Because the legend is not the same on each map, whenever you open a new one you have to learn what this particular one is going to tell you.

READING THE LEGEND

Let's look at the legend, or explanation of contents, of the map. Every symbol has been meticulously listed together with its meaning, obviously by some highly detail-oriented person. Skip over the first few lines, which show you various roads, main or secondary or other, until you get to the marking for a trail. There may be more than one kind of trail shown. These are what you will be looking for in planning your walk. They are usually shown as broken lines or dots and are extremely faint when printed on a map that is covered with all sorts of shadings and other markings, including over-all contour lines. Sometimes, looking at a survey map I am convinced that it was planned in order to give the least access to the information presented. Occasionally you'll spot a marvelous path on the map, clearly marked and uncomplicated. Look again: it's probably a boundary line or a river or a four-lane highway that you're looking at. The path you want is going to be indicated with the faintest dots on the map.

WHY LOOK AT ALL THOSE LITTLE SYMBOLS?

In general, most of them will be irrelevant to you. But if you're not sure of where you are, you'll be grateful to see that the little black square on the map is the farmhouse off to your left. Or if you're planning a walk in a rainy season, you may want to take the path that avoids what is marked as a marsh, according to the symbol in the legend. I'm often amazed at the extreme care with which the map-maker marked the salient points on a survey map.

So the answer to the question is that the little scratches, pictures, dots and pyramids on the map will help you to orient yourself during a hike. And they may help you from going astray if the regional trail markers didn't do a good job (or didn't even start, as in England).

SCALE

To work out a route, the first thing that you want to find out is the scale of the map, so that you can gauge distance accurately. The most detailed (or "large scale") maps, such as some of the Ordnance Survey maps in England, give two and a half inches to every mile (or four centimeters to every kilometer, or 1:25,000). In fact my map of the Mount Washington Area in New Hampshire is 1:20,000, or three inches to the mile—an even larger scale. Less detailed ("small scale") but still perfectly usable are the maps made on a scale of roughly one inch to one mile. It's possible that only smaller scale maps are available for the area where you'll be walking. At a park rangers office you may be given a sketch showing paths, which is much less detailed than most topographical maps, but that may be all you can get.

Once you know the scale, you can work out distance relatively easily. As paths are seldom straight, you can't just place a ruler down and measure. But you can approximate. You can use a curve meter, one of those handy gadgets with a wheel at the tip that enable you to measure the length of the path on the map. Once you have the length you can multiply the number of inches according to the scale and come up with an approximate distance in miles. More primitive, but still practical, take a length of string, twist it along the marked path on the map and measure the length of string used. Then multiply.

Getting Used to the Map

It takes a while to feel comfortable reading maps. Even if you're used to ordinary city maps or road maps and know how to navigate using them, you'll find reading a topographical map a bit of a challenge. This map, after all, shows dimensions, gives you an understanding of the lay of the land, so you're reading height into what you see on a flat surface. Once you get the hang of it, you'll find the map is truly a good friend.

Take your map with you always and check it every once in a while. Do you see where the new path comes in at the left? Can you find the crossing of the stream and the turn in the path? Estimate the distance and height that you've reached and check later to see if you worked it out correctly. Make reading the map second nature to you. Figure out which mountains you see around you. Working out their names helps to orient yourself. These exercises are useful but don't become bogged down in it—go on and enjoy your walk!

A Sample Map

On the next page is a small section of a topographical map of the area around Mount Washington in New Hampshire. Let's use this as an example of the various useful features the map presents.

1 This is the **Legend**. Here you see the kinds of symbols used on this particular map. This is not a complete listing of all the possible markings shown in a Legend. And in fact not all the symbols shown here are used in the little section that we're using as a sample. You won't find the bracketed items on our map.

2 The **Scale** is shown at the bottom. In making measurements to see approximately how far you'll be walking, take a ruler and measure the length of a mile or half mile. Make sure that you start from the zero and not from the beginning of the line! In this particular example, 0.5 mile is about one and a half inches, so we know that every mile on the ground is about three inches on the map, quite a large scale. The scale also shows that on this map the **distance between contours** corresponds with fifty feet in height.

3 This is the **Declination Diagram**. You may remember from some long-ago class in geography that the magnetic north (MN) is not precisely where the geographic north (GN) lies. This diagram—and it is shown on most topographical maps—indicates the difference, in degrees, between where the north pole is and where the magnetic north lies. This angle varies from map to map, depending on how far east or west you are. The line pointing to the star on the diagram shows the north according to the grid on the map, slightly different again. The right-hand vertical border of this map is a line on the grid,

MAP READING

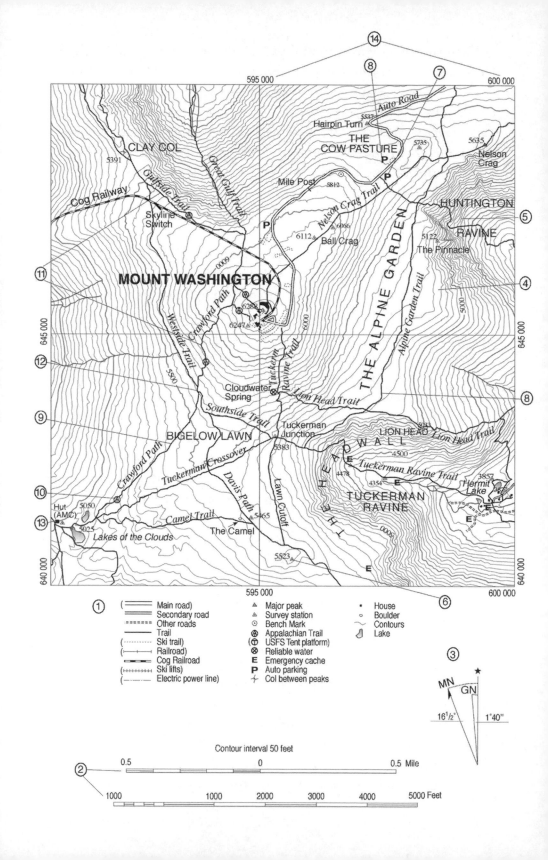

representing longitude. We'll say more about the angle of declination when we talk about the compass.

4 Now look at the **contours** that are shown. As you move on the ground from what's shown on the map as one contour line to another, you ascend (or descend) fifty feet. The further apart these lines appear on the map, the gentler the slope. Look at the area where *"Alpine Garden Trail"* is printed. We can assume that it's quite flat there, given the space between contour lines near the letters *"rde"* of *"Garden."* You'll find that every tenth line is printed in darker ink. These are **index contours** and if you let your finger follow one around on the map, you'll come to a number showing the height (in feet or meters) of that contour. It's easier to count the little faint lines when you know how many there are between each darker one.

5 The contour lines that we see here are very close to each other. It is clear that this represents very **steep terrain**. If you are planning a walk, take such a cluster of contour lines into account. Depending on your condition, you might want to avoid such a path. In this particular case, you could also have seen from the name of the place—Huntington Ravine—that it's a very steep area. But the name doesn't always give it away. If you were by any chance going cross country without a trail, you'd want to avoid this type of terrain.

6 The little triangle indicates a peak. You can see them in various places on the map. The height (5,523 feet) is given next to it. As you can see, the Davis path skirts the peak and doesn't go quite to the summit. Not all mountain walks take in the peaks. The path often makes use of a col, or lower point between peaks, to lead hikers over a mountain ridge if it makes more sense.

7 Wherever you see a **P** on a map there's a parking lot. Let's say that someone (not you!) decides to drive partway up the mountain and then park and walk up the rest of the way. If you want to know how far their walk will be from the lot, measure the real distance on the map from the **P** to the top of Mount Washington (using either technique mentioned above) and you'll find that it's a little over two inches. So the walk would only be about three-quarters of a mile.

MAP READING

8 Now, the question is, how much of a climb would it be from the parking lot to the summit of Mount Washington? First establish how high the parking lot is. To do this, locate the contour that the **P** is on. Now follow that contour straight down the page (south) until you are under (to the right of) the number 6000 on the index contour (near the words Ravine Trail). Count the contour lines between (there should be five); multiply them by 50 (feet) and you will see that the contour of the parking lot is at 5,750 feet. So you know that your friend in the car will have to walk uphill three-quarters of a mile and up just under 550 feet. You'll notice that the road itself was built partially around the contours in a way that would lessen the gradient.

9 Here you see the marking for a **trail**. There are a large number of them on this little section. On other maps they might be represented by dotted or broken lines.

10 Here's the Appalachian Trail (AT); you can see the symbol.

11 Using this symbol, you can trace the AT up the Crawford Trail, to the top of Mount Washington and then follow its course down off the mountain in a different way, finally joining up with the Gulfside Trail.

12 At this spot the Crawford Path crosses the Westside Trail and also meets up with the Southside Trail at almost the same point. If you were walking and in doubt about your location, you would have been able to establish exactly where you were when you came across the conjunction of these paths. You could also tell what height you're at when you reach that juncture, again by checking contours. By counting back two contours, you can see the index contour marked 5500. As each counter is 50 feet from the next, you know that you are standing at 5,600 feet. You also know that you have almost 700 feet to climb up till you get to the top of Mount Washington.

13 The little black square indicates a building. In this case it is the AMC hut at the Lakes of the Clouds. You've arrived at your destination for the night!

14 These are **coordinates**. They are lines that run on the north-south and east-west parallels. People sometimes give the coordi-

nates to pinpoint their specific location (instead of, for example, giving a compass reading). The numbers given here are at 5,000-foot intervals. This means that each partition on the map is a little under a mile square. Knowing this can be helpful to you in working out rough distances.

Using a Compass

Hikers don't ordinarily use a compass unless there's a problem in orienting themselves. If you're on a clear path and feel that you know where you are, there's no need to pull out your compass. But do keep it in a handy place, ready for use. With luck, certainly on your early walks, and in much of your day walking, you'll never take it out of your pocket.

When Would You Take Out a Compass?

A compass cannot tell you where you are. It can only tell you where north is and the rest is up to you. Your job is to coordinate the spot on the map where you are standing, with the compass point to gain maximum understanding of your geographical location. There are a few cases where a compass would be useful.

> *It may be that you will hike on endless paths, up and down countless mountains, and never need a compass.*

1. You're caught in a fog on top of a mountain and can't see the valleys below. There are two paths going down and only one will take you to the right place. From the map you know that you want the path heading east. Use your compass to work out direction and then pick the eastern path.
2. You'd like to get your bearings after having lost the path. You know that you should be heading west, but the sun is overhead or covered by thick cloud and you can't work out the direction. Your compass will help.
3. There are some mountains off to the left and you're not sure which ones they are. Lots of mountains are shown on your map, with their names, but unless you know which way you are facing you can't tell which ones you're looking at.

4. In general, any time that you are unsure of which path to take or how to proceed, your compass will be an all-important tool.

Let's Look at a Compass

There are a few basic elements to know about a compass. Then you have to get used to coordinating your reading of the compass with what you see on the map.

COMPONENT PARTS OF A COMPASS

You can still buy a very simple compass that costs little and can accurately indicate north. This is adequate for most functions you're likely to need. The most basic one looks like a pocket watch with a single free-floating pointer and N, E, S, W marked on the dial.

But the standard compass sold today in outdoor sports stores is a step above that. Slightly more complex, the preferred compass offers more precision and certainly more ease in coordinating your findings with a map. This compass is in the form of a directional needle in a circular piece of plastic set on a flat rectangle. Let's look at the rectangle, or **base plate**, first. It has a number of features:

- The *direction-of-travel arrow*. It is imprinted in the plastic above the dial.
- Sometimes there is a *magnifying lens* set in the base plate, which can be very useful, given the tiny and unclear markings that we have just seen on the map.
- On the outside edge there are markings for a *centimeter or inch scale* to coordinate with the map scale.
- The base plate is clear plastic so that if you place it on a map you can see through to the markings.

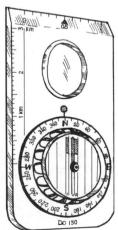

On the **dial** we see:

- The *compass needle*. The needle is made of two colors and the red (or gold or other attention-getting color) end is the part of the needle that seeks north.

- The *compass housing* is a rotatable dial that has the 360 degrees of a circle marked on its rim. Also on the rim are the initials for north, south, east and west, each separated by 90 degrees.
- There is a fixed *orienting arrow* under the needle, pointing towards the N on the dial permanently.
- In the background of the compass housing are parallel lines called *orienting lines* which can be used to align your position on a map.

Using a Compass

Figuring out direction alone with a compass is very straightforward. If you have a compass in the house, take it out now and follow this while looking at your compass.

First find north. Well, the compass needle does that for you. The red end automatically seeks the north (unless some powerful magnetic force nearby affects it). Wherever the red tip of the arrow points, that is the magnetic north. Line up your compass so that all directional indicators—the orienting arrow on the dial, the direction-of-travel arrow on the rectangle and the red-tipped compass needle are all pointing in the same direction—north.

THE OLD-FASHIONED WAY

The least complicated method of using a compass for direction is perfectly accurate. Locate magnetic north on the simplest of compasses by seeing where the arrow is pointing. As you know that the opposite direction is south and that east and west are to the right and left, at right-angles, you can work out everything from that, using your eye. It's very straightforward, reliable, and simple.

MORE "HIGH TECH" WAY

The more complex plastic compass we're discussing can help you to locate very specific directions quite simply and more accurately. For example, if you want to work out where you should head if you know you need a northeasterly direction proceed as follows:

1. Find where northeast is permanently marked on the dial (between N and E, at about 45 degrees). Don't pay any attention to where the magnetic needle is pointing.

2. Now turn the dial so that the northeast spot (45) is aligned with the direction-of-travel arrow on the base plate at the top.

3. Next, turn the entire compass (not the dial) until you align the north-seeking end of the needle with the orienting arrow below it in the dial. The needle itself is, of course, still pointing to the north.

4. Take a look at the direction-of-travel arrow in the base plate. It is now pointing toward the northeast, which is where you want to go.

Try this exercise a few times at home to get used to doing it. It's best in the beginning if you already know where north is so that you can corroborate your compass findings with what you know experientially about directions.

We are not discussing cross-country trekking here, so I am assuming that you are using the compass to determine which path to take and not how to pick your way through the wilderness.

But if you have somehow lost the path altogether and are just aiming toward a particular direction in order to pick up another trail or a road that you think is there, you should keep spotting salient points in the landscape—a hill, a boulder, or some other local feature—that are in the northeasterly direction to keep yourself on target. Walk toward the boulder or hill and then to the next spot along the same line. Then you won't have to keep looking down at your compass all the time.

Using Your Compass with the Map

If you know approximately where you are and know roughly where you are heading, but can't see your way there because of fog or an unclear path, you can work with compass and map together.

1. Put the map down on a flat surface (if it's raining it should be in the plastic map case) or hold it level in your hands and align the compass in the following way.

2. Using the straight long edge of the rectangular base, place it on the map like a ruler in a way that you connect the point where you are now standing with the point that you're heading

for. The direction-of-travel arrow should be pointing toward your goal on the map. Now we have to translate that information to the real situation on the ground.

3. Keep the compass in that position on the map. Now swivel the dial to align the parallel lines inside the dial (orienting lines) with the grid on your map (these are north-south lines). Make sure that you have positioned the map so that north is at the top.

4. Now, turn the map and the entire compass (not the dial itself) until the north-pointing needle is aligned with the orienting lines and the orienting arrow inside the dial. (As you are holding the compass against the map, those orienting lines are still parallel to the grid on the map, facing north.) You've now oriented your map and compass in the right direction.

5. Once they are aligned, take the compass off the map. You can now simply follow the direction-of-travel arrow toward your destination. Be careful not to rotate the dial while you are walking and keep the red point of the needle floating over the orienting arrow. The angle (azimuth) between the needle and the direction-of-travel arrow will thus remain constant.

USING A COMPASS

A good friend, who ordinarily never uses a compass, found it necessary to take one out when he and a companion were crossing a high glacier and found themselves caught in dense cloud. Relying on the compass and their knowledge of the map, they charted a course across the glacier toward a hut that they knew should be there, but finally gave up in despair. They spent the night huddled out in the extreme cold, keeping themselves warm by heating snow for hot drinks. In the morning, they discovered that the hut they were seeking was a few feet away. The compass had done its job—but they hadn't known it.

Inaccuracies: Angle of Declination

While all this seems relatively straightforward once you have practiced it a bit with your own compass, there is an inherent inaccuracy in the procedure. Do you remember when we looked at the map earlier in this chapter and saw the declination diagram? The angle shown—and it varies, as we noted, with your geographic location—represents the discrepancy between what we shall call true north (or geographic north) and magnetic north. In serious navigating, this angle has to be taken into account and the direction of the north must be adjusted to indicate geographic north rather than magnetic north. On the map that we looked at in this chapter there's a relatively small difference, but in other locations it might be quite substantial. If you're just trying to obtain a general orientation you may be able to make do with the approximate directions you're getting from your compass. If it's important to get an absolutely reliable reading, then you'll have to check your topographical map, find the angle of declination (azimuth), and adjust your compass by that many degrees.

TO ADJUST FOR DECLINATION

Your compass measures the 360 degrees of the circle. So if you see that the magnetic north is 16 degrees to the west of geographic north (as on our sample map), you'll add 16 degrees to the zero at N on the dial. The basic principle is to line up your compass so that the compass needle is pointing to the magnetic north (as always) and the direction-of-travel arrow and the orienting arrow are both aligned with it. Everything is thus pointing to the magnetic north. Now turn the whole compass (not the dial) until compass needle is pointing to the declination angle that the map shows. In this case, that means that the needle should point to 16 degrees on the dial. Now the direction-of-travel arrow is left of the magnetic needle and is pointing to the geographical north. (The angle between the red needle pointing to the magnetic north on the one hand and the N on the dial—together with the direction-of-travel arrow—is the declination.) As a rule of thumb, if the magnetic north lies so many degrees to the west of the geographic north you add that number of degrees to the zero and if it's to the east, you subtract the number of degrees of declination from 360.

An alternative to this system is to set your compass to the declination at the beginning of a walk and avoid making adjustments later.

A further complication will be briefly mentioned: the declination in any given place changes from year to year. So although this has all sounded quite scientific, it isn't at all, because your map may already be out of date. While some map makers give additional information on the annual change in the number of degrees of declination, a great number do not. My advice: stay out of trouble! Stick to the path. Follow the markings. Check with your map and don't get lost.

Figuring Out Where You Are with Common Sense
With a decent map and common sense you can work out your location indirectly. Here's an example:

You're on a mountainside and wonder how far you've climbed. There are no indications from the map—crossing another path, passing a stream, going by a farm—that you can use to establish where you are. But across from you, halfway up a mountain to the north, you can see a building (or some other landmark) that's marked on the map. It's at eye level with you. As you know that that object—according to the map contour—is at 2,150 feet, you can safely assume that you're at about 2,000 feet as well. Knowing this, you can figure out roughly where you are on the map.

Another help in locating your position, besides the suggestions given here and in section 12 on the map, is to use the Legend again. You'll notice that there's a symbol for something called a "bench mark." Bench marks are the little round metal disks that you occasionally find embedded in the ground when you're hiking on a trail. They've been placed there by people surveying the territory. If you have only a rough idea of where you are but come across a benchmark in the ground, you can check your map for the location.

Other Aids
The truth is that you can spend a lot of time walking without ever needing anything except a map and, possibly, a compass. Other aids (as mentioned in Chapter 7) can add to your enjoyment but are not necessary.

Altimeter
An altimeter tells you what height you're at. This is useful if you want to know how far you've climbed or how much farther you have to go

until you get to the top. Some are inexpensive, others very pricey. For a non-professional walker, the lower range is adequate. We rarely use an altimeter, though in the chapter on hiking in America you'll see an example of when you might want to. It's only in the Himalayas—away from any ordinary path markings—that we have found it nice to have one, though not necessary. In Chapter 9 you'll find an explanation of why some people like to carry an altimeter.

I enjoy knowing how far up we've climbed because I enjoy toting up facts. If you're hiking with kids they may get a kick out of checking altitude, even on the most straightforward path.

Check the instructions on the packaging to adjust your altimeter for use.

GPS

There are now wonderful devices that use the Global Positioning System to pinpoint exactly where you are with tremendous precision, whether you're driving on an unfamiliar road or hiking on an unfamiliar path. Here, too, if you like high-tech products you'll enjoy using one of these. They're expensive and certainly not necessary for ordinary day-walking. But if you own one anyway, take it along and have fun! Some of these devices can be carried in a pocket, others are installed as part of an advanced watch.

Clearly, this gadget would be of tremendous benefit if you were truly lost although even with this system the information may not be precisely accurate for your needs.

Summing Up

The most important information in this chapter concerns map-reading. You'll want to understand the details on a map well enough to pick out a good route. But in the beginning of your mountain career you're unlikely to need to perfect any of these skills. You're not planning to start out in the wilderness, nor to do cross-country trekking without the help of marked trails. So don't worry if the information here seems unduly complicated at the moment.

What to Wear

Chapter 5

In some ways, what you wear in the mountains is very unimportant. Unlike skiing or even tennis, fashion is not a high priority for walkers. No one cares whether you are color-coordinated, have logos of top sports clothing manufacturers or look like a model. So if you want to look terrific on the trail, by all means go ahead. But if you choose to be very laid-back about what you wear because this is, after all, your vacation, that's just fine. In mountain areas—the villages where you'll be staying overnight—people tend toward the informal, even in the evening in the restaurants and pubs. It's not like après-ski.

If anything, there's sometimes a reverse attitude on the part of some walkers. I was off to a conference a number of years ago, which by a happy circumstance was taking place in a village in the Austrian Alps. I packed some walking clothes, just in case. I remarked to my husband, who was watching me, that it was too bad my jacket looked fairly rundown. It had definitely seen better days. But he remarked that, on the contrary, the jacket looked marvelous—as if it had gone through plenty of walking, which it had. For him, a worn jacket, scuffed boots, were a badge of honor. I think that lots of mountain lovers feel that way and cling fondly to worn-out clothing associated with long and pleasant meanderings.

Boots

Let's talk about feet first, because your boots are the most important item of apparel in the mountains. Without good footwear you'll get tired more easily, possibly be in pain, and run the risk of losing your footing on slippery surfaces. They are your lifeline to a successful walk.

Why do you need boots? Why not sneakers? It is true that you can see people in the mountains walking in various styles of sneakers and they seem to be doing all right. For the ordinary walk it is possible that a pair of sneakers will be perfectly satisfactory, as long as they have good tread. But when you go out in the mountains, you always have to think of the worst-case scenario. And that includes the possibility that you will run into rain, puddles, mud (or snow, if you're high enough), or slippery rocks or tree roots. In these circumstances, there is nothing as good as a pair of thick, sturdy leather hiking boots that go up to your ankles.

Last spring we took a long walk in the Chilterns, the rolling hills outside London. The weather was magnificent for walking: bright, clear, sunny. But part of the path we had chosen coincided with a bridle path and, though we didn't run into any horses, we were very aware that they used the path: it was totally churned up and had become very muddy. It would have been extremely uncomfortable walking through the mud in sneakers, and at the end of the day we would probably have just thrown them out. But with boots on, who cared?

If you're just trying out mountain walking and want to get a taste of it without spending too much money, do some walking in a nearby place with whatever comfortable, safe, well-tread shoes you own. But if you're planning a good walking week or two for your next vacation, buying a pair of boots will be a worthwhile investment. And they will last for years.

As I explained in the first chapter, choosing your boots takes time. Important decisions have to be made and you shouldn't try to buy boots when you are in a hurry.

First, find a store that sells boots, lots of them. Don't go to a shoe store that happens to have one or two hiking boots in their stock. Your best option is to go to a good sports store in your area that has a boot section or a shoe store that has a wide selection of boots. But if you live far from a decent shop, you might want to look into other possibilities. Getting boots through mail order is possible, though not ideal. It's good to be able to try on a few boots, one after another, to make sure you're making the best choice. But if your options are limited, make do with what is available, whether that means a lesser store or mail order, if you're sure that you can return the purchase. There is also the option of looking for boots in the region where you'll be doing your mountain walking. It's common to find the supplies you need right in the mountain area, whether it's in Montana or in a Swiss village or in the English

Lake District. But you should make sure that there are boot shops and that they carry your size if it's an unusual one, or you'll be stuck without boots. Once in the English Lake District I actually rented a pair of hiking boots when I saw signs that my own boots were on the verge of falling apart.

If you buy your boots in a store that's geared toward outdoor sports the chances are that they'll have a better selection and that they'll have sales people who understand the needs of a walker. Every time I've bought boots I've had the feeling that the person helping me has done it, been there, knows what to look for in terms of comfort and durability. And they're usually very patient, because they understand that you've absolutely got to find the right fit. Some of the larger stores, whether in New York or Seattle, will have some kind of incline, a sort of miniature mountain, that you can use to test the boots for comfort, see where your toes get to when pointing downhill, and so on.

For a first pair of boots, avoid getting leather that is too stiff. Walking will be much easier in boots that are not too high or too inflexible. Does the boot top hit you ankle bone in an uncomfortable way? Is there plenty of room for your toes? Remember that when it's warm, feet swell. Is the inner sole well padded and cushioned? Is the boot wide enough at the widest part of your foot? Aim at feeling completely comfortable in the boots that you select in the store. Don't listen to advice that the boots have to be "broken in" or that the pressure on your toe will disappear once the leather softens. *Do not select boots on the basis of looks.*

Firmer soles on boots are only necessary if you are planning to use certain kinds of crampons, (the metal spikes that clamp onto the bottom of the boot to provide a secure foothold on snow or ice). But this is a specialized need and unless you feel comfortable in the firmer boot, avoid it in a first pair. Stores are now showing hiking boots that look a

> "My first impression of Beck had not been favorable . . . but the better I got to know him, the more he earned my respect. Even though his inflexible new boots had chewed his feet into hamburger, Beck kept hobbling upward, day in and day out, scarcely mentioning what must have been horrific pain."
> —*Jon Krakauer,* Into Thin Air

WHAT TO WEAR

bit like ski boots and are made of hard synthetic material. They are fully waterproof, but I shy away from these for reasons of comfort, flexibility and a need for the shoe to "breathe."

The market also offers flexible synthetic material imitating leather, or combinations of leather and canvas. One advantage is that they are lighter than many leather boots. But a certain amount of weight in a boot can be an advantage—it gives you a sense of ballast and stability on rough terrain. Go into a sports store in Switzerland, ask about non-leather climbing boots or leather boots that are lined with water-proofed material, and you will get very negative comments: not comfortable, your feet sweat too much, not what the guides use. Personally, I stick with leather-lined leather boots and love them. But I stay away from inflexible boots for ordinary mountain walking, preferring the slightly lighter and more flexible kind.

When you try on boots, keep in mind what kind of socks you'll be wearing when you are walking. Don't try on a pair of boots over stockings just because you've just come from work and are wearing heels. Bring the kind of socks with you that you'll wear for walking. Or discuss it with the sales people in the boot department; they'll probably lend you socks to try on with the boots. If the boots feel fine with those socks, buy a few pairs so that you can be sure of a comfortable fit.

Personally, I wear medium-thick cotton socks (really, tennis-socks) under my boots, preferring something simple and not too bulky, and I try on a new boot with that kind of sock. Occasionally, in really cold weather, I wear thicker cotton socks with padded soles. But some walkers prefer to wear two socks, one over the other, one thick, one thin. The inner sock goes up underneath the slacks while the outer sock is then folded over the top of the boot. This gives a little more thickness between the boot and the foot and some added protection against snow getting in, if you're walking in snow. In Switzerland and Germany you'll see some people wearing long, often colorful, socks, up over the calf and then shorter walking trousers that button just under the knee, meeting the sock. But that seems geographically specific and I haven't seen it out of the Alpine regions recently. The main thing is to suit the socks to the boot, and to have enough so that you always have a clean pair of socks to start the walk.

The reason that it's best to buy boots near home is that you will then be able to wear them in long before you actually take them on a serious hike.

And I can't stress how important this is. Good leather boots will adjust to your feet; they're pliable and should become more and more comfortable as you wear them. By walking them in, you can detect possible problems in advance. The boot may rub here or there after you've brought it home and by softening it up, you'll avoid future trouble. Once you've got your new boots, put them on at home and walk around inside the house with them every evening for an hour or two, making sure that they're comfortable. Then go outside for a short walk here and there, until you're sure that you're happy in them. Never put on a brand new pair of boots for a long walk. It is possible that the fit is so good that everything will go well. (I was lucky that way with my first pair of boots.) But if that doesn't happen you will spend a long time regretting it. So the wearing-in process shouldn't be skipped or shortened.

Outerwear

Let me start by saying that no single item that you wear for mountain walking should be big and bulky. Once you start walking uphill—often within fifteen minutes—you generate quite a lot of body heat and you will hate yourself for having worn a heavy jacket that you now have to carry for the rest of the day.

What you want to wear on the outside is a shell, an anorak, a windbreaker. It can be unlined or lightly lined but the important characteristic is that the jacket should be a good shield against wind and rain.

I used to wear a cotton or cotton/synthetic blend jacket that was water resistant but not waterproof and then had to carry along some kind of waterproof garment—a plastic poncho or rainwear—to put on over my jacket when it started to rain. But now that you can buy jackets made with Gore-Tex, I have one less garment to take along. Fabric treated with Gore-Tex is waterproof (as nylon rainwear is) but has the added benefit that it still "breathes." Today's waterproof anoraks are now generally made of a polyester that seems to have the best characteristics of cotton and are treated with Gore-Tex. They combine maximum comfort with maximum protection.

Again, if you have a jacket that you love and you don't want to buy a new one, then make do with that and carry some kind of nylon/plastic rainwear. But you will find that while you're keeping the rain off, you're perspiring so much that your clothes will be soaked anyway. If you're

WHAT TO WEAR

walking in an area or a season where there's no chance of rain whatsoever, then you don't have to worry about the extra layer.

In Selecting an Anorak, Keep the Following Point in Mind:

1. *It should be roomy* enough to allow for several layers of clothing, including a heavy sweater.
2. *It should have pockets.* You'll need things on the way that you can get to easily, while you're wearing the jacket, things like tissues, toilet paper, maybe tickets for a cable car or bus. (They'll have to be transferred when you take off your jacket unless you can easily get it out of your backpack.) My anorak has inside pockets as well. If I'm on a long trek, I may want to carry my passport or credit card in there, safe from rain and far from pockets that I will rummage in more often.
3. To repeat, *the fabric should "breathe."*
4. Jackets that pull over your head are not as convenient to use as those that are open in the front. The latter also gives you the choice of wearing it open or closed. If there's a choice, *get a jacket with a hood.*

Rainwear

I'd like to say another word about rainwear, for a few reasons:

- If you plan to use a poncho—one of those plastic capes, usually inexpensive, that covers all of you down to the knees— you will have the disadvantage of that build-up of body heat I mentioned but the advantage of a garment that also covers your backpack, thus keeping everything inside dry. There are other ways to deal with the problem of a backpack in the rain, but I'll be talking about that later in this chapter and in Chapter 6.
- Even if you have an anorak that's waterproof, you may still need other rain gear. We routinely carry waterproof pants with us if we're walking anyplace where there could be heavy rain. They don't weigh a lot and you feel that they're well worth the trouble if you're ever caught in a downpour with a long way to go.

- Waterproof pants generally have an elastic waistband, no buttons, no pockets, no nonsense (no style either!). But they do have zippers at the bottom of each leg so that you can put them on over your boots. The last thing you want to do is to take off your boots in the rain because you can't pull on the waterproof pants over them. (It's hard enough without doing that!)
- If you're in doubt about taking waterproof pants along, think of how you'll feel wearing wet slacks that are clinging to your legs as you walk, possibly for hours. We walk so often in the English mountains that it's unthinkable not to take along all the rain gear you need. And while we've been very lucky with the weather over the years, there are certainly days that I can remember when we walked for six or seven hours in the rain, trying to get from a village in one valley, over the mountain to a village in the next.

Clothing

What do we wear underneath all that protection? I'll give some general ideas here because I don't know if you'll be walking in hot dry places, in cold weather, or what. So here is the most important principle: **dress in layers.**

On a visit to Arizona, en route to the Grand Canyon, we stopped at a little waterfall to see the view and ended up looking at jewelry that a number of Indians had laid out on display on the ground. I looked at one of the women, sitting there on a blanket next to her wares in the very cold February air and said to her, "I guess you've got a lot of layers on." She smiled back and said, "Like an onion." And that's what you should do.

When you leave for your walk in the morning, assuming that it's still early and chilly, you'll be wearing an anorak. Under that, you will probably want to wear either a sweatshirt or a sweater and then a t-shirt, which is what you will probably end up walking in for the rest of the day, once you warm up.

As you walk, your body heats up. You'll want to shed your anorak now. That will probably be your first stop in the walk (aside from photo stops): to take off your jacket. If you're in a rush to go on, you may just tie it around your waist. Otherwise, fold it into your backpack.

Later, as it gets warmer, you'll take off your sweatshirt and put that into the backpack as well. For the rest of the morning, weather permitting, you'll be walking in your t-shirt, or something similar with long sleeves if you prefer. Even if the outside air is quite cold you'll be amazed at how little you'll wear while you're walking uphill.

It's not uncommon to find yourself in very light clothing surrounded by people in warm jackets. I remember one incident when we walked up from Zermatt to the Gornergrat, a magnificent five-hour walk ending with one of the finest views in the Alps, at a summit 5,000 feet above the starting point. On a steep, steady walk like that we climbed the last hundred-yard slope to the observatory at the top still wearing in lightweight shirts. The famous Gornergrat cog railway hauls large numbers of day visitors up the mountain, so there were plenty of people strolling around at 10,000 feet altitude, taking pictures, looking through binoculars, warmly dressed in padded jackets. But we were still warm as toast from our climb and, in contrast, dressed for a mild summer day.

The change comes when you stop, either for lunch or for a rest. That's when you have to be careful. Don't sit around in just your t-shirt because you were so warm a few minutes ago. Open that backpack and take out your sweatshirt, which is right on top. That's why it's there. And if it's cold enough, out comes the anorak as well. All during the day you may find yourself taking it off and putting it on. That's fine. You don't want to get chilled and you're carrying clothing for that very purpose. When you get started again, the same peeling process begins once more.

Whatever you wear, your t-shirt, sweatshirt, and jacket should be comfortable and not confining. The same goes for the pants that you wear. Don't wear tight-fitting jeans. You'll hate yourself later. You may look terrific in them, but your legs will end up uncomfortable and sweaty. Get a pair of loose-fitting jeans, cargo pants, or other easy-fit slacks. In shops specializing in outdoor sportswear you can also find pull-on hiking pants, that have loose elastic at the waist and the ankles, trim and very useful. Another choice that is available are zip-off convertible pants—they have a zipper near the knee, enabling the walker to go out in the cool morning in long pants and, in the heat of the day, end up wearing shorts. Whatever the style, I'm in favor of pockets in pants: you never know what you might want to carry for easy access.

Some people (men and women) prefer to wear shorts when they're walking, but I would not wear shorts unless I was very sure that the path is clear—that is, without jagged stones, stinging nettles, or other prickly plants. And be sure that there are no snakes in the area. You could regret wearing shorts very easily, given the possible obstacles, so give a thought to it before you dress for the day.

The best thing for the mountains is to pull out some old, unfashionable pants that you wore once upon a time, maybe when you weighed a few pounds more, and some worn-out tops that should have been given away already but are still in the back of the drawer. Those would be great for hiking.

I tend to wear cotton when I'm walking. It's clean, cool, comfortable, feels good, and breathes. Some climbers today prefer synthetic fabrics because of their ability to absorb body moisture and then dry out again. This is a question of personal comfort and you should try them out and decide for yourself. Fashions in these matters, as in certain kinds of medical advice, vary from period to period and often return to the original point. You'll have to establish your own comfort level.

The same goes with a hat. If you want to shade your face or protect your head from the sun, you should definitely wear a hat with a brim or peak when you go walking. If you're not used to wearing a hat and usually go out in the sun without it, then stick to your usual policy (unless you are planning to walk in a very hot area, such as the tropics or sub-tropics).

Underwear

Just a few words about what you might want to wear under everything else.

Some bra companies have a range of sports bras. You may want to look into these. They tend to hold you in a firmer way and are sensible.

However, you may have very comfortable bras that are not your best and that you won't mind wearing while you're perspiring. This is usually my first choice. Bring a few along on your trip, rinse them out in the evening when you get in and have them clean to use for the next morning's walk. Whether it's a sports bra or an ordinary one, it should give you adequate support when you're walking.

Avoid wearing clothing close to your skin that has a residue of perspiration: it can cause chafing and ultimately a great deal of discomfort.

There is also wonderful thermal underwear available in a variety of stores that specialize in sports wear as well as in some department stores. For the ordinary walk, whether in the Rockies or in the Alps, you will not want to wear thermal underwear: it's too warm. But you may find it useful for the evenings when you're back from your walk and strolling around a cold village, looking in the shop windows. I particularly like the silk kind, long sleeved (and long legged, if you want to wear something under your slacks as well). They're comfortable and warm but light at the same time. If you're camping out, or on a trek, thermal underwear is invaluable and I've gladly worn it to bed—that is, inside my sleeping bag—and been very grateful to have it. It's so thin and light that it's no effort to carry and well worth it if you're facing icy temperatures at night.

The Backpack

If you already have some kind of backpack in your home and it is comfortable to carry, that should be fine. We are talking here about a backpack (or rucksack) on the bigger end of what is called a daypack, on the assumption that, at least in the beginning, you will be completing your round trip in a single day. Even if you plan to walk from place to place for a few days, a small backpack should be sufficient unless, of course, you're camping.

> **TERMINOLOGY:** Manufacturers give their own terms to various gradations of packs. I'm using the generic term in the text, but this is the more technical terminology:
>
> *Daypack.* Capacity: 1,800–2,000 cubic inches. Empty weight: weighs 1½ – 2 lb. This is the kind of pack for a typical day hike, carrying just enough for all-weather needs.
>
> *Rucksack.* Capacity: 3,000 cubic inches. Empty weight: 2½ – 3 lb. This larger version of a daypack is useful if you are carrying extra gear—either clothing for someone else walking with you (e.g., a child) or if the weather threatens to be extremely volatile, or if you're toting enough clothing for a few days.
>
> *Backpack.* Capacity: 3,900–8,000 cubic inches. Empty weight: 5–8 lb. This very serious kind of pack is for long-distance walkers and trekkers. You'd never want it on the average climb.

What I look for in a backpack (as in clothes) is comfort, first and foremost. You don't want to walk with something on your back that is unwieldy, overbalanced, digging in at your shoulders or causing you back trouble. So in buying one, it is important to try the backpack on, not just look at it. There are some backpacks that are specifically designed for women, in that the straps sit differently on your shoulders and rest under your arms in the front at a different angle. Ask if the store has anything of this kind as you may prefer this style. But I have generally found that all-round ("men's"?—not really!) backpacks can be perfectly comfortable. Just find the one that sits on you suitably, making sure to adjust the shoulder straps and the strap at the waist for the right length and size. When you're wearing a filled backpack, you'll want to ensure that some of the weight is taken off your shoulders and

WHAT TO WEAR

shifts to your hips. Adjusting the straps and fastening the strap at the waist will help you to do this.

For a daypack, you will probably want a soft pack without a frame. But if you are buying something that, in the future, you plan to use for longer hikes, camping or treks, you might want to consider one of the smaller rucksacks with a frame. These can distribute the weight of the pack more evenly, causing less pressure on your back. Certainly, if you ever have back problems—and so many people do—you have to give as much thought and time to selecting your backpack as your boots. Carrying a pack, if you're not used to it, can be trying when you've got the added stress of walking uphill. So it's best to have a well balanced pack, keeping the weight to a minimum.

Don't let yourself be talked into a rucksack that you're not sure of. There have been so many advances in the design of these packs that sometimes some very odd ones are produced. A number of years ago my husband treated himself to a new backpack and became convinced that the way it was designed—a frame that extended up above the backpack behind his head—would alleviate a lot of the pressure on his back. This was for a walk that we were taking over a period of a few days and he would be carrying a fairly heavy load. In fact, the pack was quite successful in distributing the weight, but because it extended so high above his head, my husband found himself in a very precarious position every time he had to duck past a boulder or an overhanging tree on the narrow and precipitous path. The extension made it very difficult to keep his balance. I, with my ordinary soft pack, had no trouble at all and had to keep waiting for him to make his way around obstacles.

In hunting for a good backpack, look for pockets and zipper compartments. Some backpacks are so streamlined that they've got no outside pockets at all. I wouldn't take one of those. You need an outside pocket for carrying a water bottle. Carrying it at the waist or hanging around your neck will become uncomfortable on a long walk. Water has to be easily accessible so that you can drink whenever you're thirsty (though you shouldn't stop to drink all the time or you won't be able to keep up a good rhythm of walking). I try to get backpacks that have pockets on either side, one for my water and the other for whatever I want to store for easy access.

Things get mixed up eas-
ily in backpacks and small
items that you might want to
reach for quickly—extra film,
a flashlight, handkerchiefs,
money, suntan lotion—should
be in an outside pocket and
not deep inside.

Besides outside pockets, you
may want a backpack that has
compartments. This is not
really necessary for a daypack,
but if you plan longer walks,
where you'll be carrying your
clothing on your back, then it
makes life much easier if you

*Another kind of backpack that has
been making an appearance in sporting good stores is the so-called
Camelbak pack. This contains a separate inner pouch (in the part nearest
your back) for water. You can fill it
with a quart, or quarts, of liquid,
depending on its volume, and have
direct access to your drink through a
tube that acts as a straw, emerging
from the backpack near your shoulder. Such a system has obvious advantages and disadvantages.*

can place certain categories of items in a particular compartment, especially if you think that you might be rummaging for something in the
dark.

Some backpacks also have lower sections that can be opened by a separate zipper. These can be useful for carrying an extra pair of shoes,
dirty laundry, or a wet towel. Again, this is not necessary for ordinary
day walking.

Because modern backpacks are often designed in a very high-tech
fashion, with all kinds of adjustments that can be made for a perfect fit,
you should make sure that you know just how it works while you're still
in the store. There are times that I think I'll have to get an engineer to
explain the workings of the back-adjustment straps once I'm struggling
with them at home!

One last note: some backpacks come with a waterproof cover, usually
neatly folded into a pocket at the bottom. Alternatively, separate covers
can also be purchased if you can find one that fits your pack. You might
consider this, if it doesn't add too much weight. In the next chapter I
will discuss other ways to protect the contents of your backpack in the
rain.

What to Put in Your Backpack and Why

Now that you have good boots and a serviceable backpack, you're almost ready to go. But as you head out on your first walk, what do you carry in the backpack? On the one hand, you have to take everything that is necessary for a day's walking and on the other hand, you don't want the backpack to be too heavy. What seems comfortably light at eight in the morning can feel like a ton after you've climbed a few thousand feet. So you want the rucksack to hold everything necessary, but not an ounce more.

Every item has a function, though you may not use it on your day's walk. Consider yourself very lucky if you've carried raingear on your back every day of your vacation and never had to use it. It's like having fire insurance.

Let's go through the contents of your backpack, what you should take and why.

Clothing

Whatever you don't actually wear, but may need later, goes into your backpack. Even on a sunny day, rain gear goes in.

Let's say that it's relatively cold and you wear a couple of layers over your t-shirt. It could take fifteen or twenty minutes to warm up enough to take one or both of these pieces of clothing off. They will then go into the backpack. If you don't want to make a real stop, you might feel comfortable tying the sleeves of the sweatshirt around your waist, but eventually you'll want to pack it away and walk comfortably. One thing that you should avoid is making frequent stops. You want to get into a rhythm and stick to it. Every stop interferes with that.

Although I said that the morning can be the coolest time of the day, you may feel colder later, when you reach the highest elevation of your walk. When you get to the summit—or the saddle—you will surely want to enjoy the view. As soon as you stop, even if you're still feeling warm from your exertions, take your sweater out of your backpack and put it on. If you've ascended to a very high point, you may want to put on every spare piece of clothing that you've brought along. This could be the place you've chosen to have a lunch break and, even with your warmer clothes on, you'll want to find a sheltered spot, out of the wind. When you get up to start your walk again, you'll begin to take off the extra clothing and return it to your backpack, either all at once or gradually.

If you're going to great heights where it could be particularly cold and windy, you will also want a scarf in your rucksack as well as gloves. Woolen gloves are less useful than leather or leather-type lined gloves which have the added advantage of being water resistant. If it ends up raining or being snowy, you'll be glad that you didn't take knitted gloves.

Another item to stow in your backpack is a cap, a warm one that comes down over the ears. Although you may not need one, it's a good thing to stuff in, particularly for high places, or if there's a sudden change in the weather. If your anorak has a hood, you may feel that it is sufficient, although it won't give you the same warmth.

And while we are talking about headgear, let me remind you about a hat. You may be a person who always wears hats in the sun, in which case, you'll have it on your head when you start your walk. Depending upon the amount of sunlight, the heat and your own preferences, you should certainly consider wearing a hat on your hike. (If this book were directed at men, I would recommend a hat strongly, especially if a person has thinning hair.)

Something else you'll want to wear, at least at times, is a pair of sunglasses. Even if you don't care to have them on all the time, bring along sunglasses in your backpack. On a snowy patch they'll protect your eyes from the glare. Some people prefer goggles, as they hold on more securely. Protecting your eyes is particularly important as it is clear that a glare can contribute to cataracts in the long run.

You may also want to bring a spare pair of dry socks, depending upon your route and the likelihood that you'll need a change. On an ordinary walk this is unnecessary. But if your socks get wet and you continue to slosh around in them, there's a good chance that you'll end up with a blister.

Packing Your Clothing

We used to just pack our clothes directly into the rucksack until a particular walk that we took in the English Lake District many years ago. We were backpacking at the time, walking from place to place and sleeping over in a different village every night. So we had more than the usual amount of clothing in our packs. On this particular vacation, we were walking from Borrowdale to Grasmere, a six- or seven-hour walk. Partway to Grasmere, we ran into rain, common enough in England. But this was not the usual Irish mist; it was a heavy downpour. We put on our anoraks and whatever rain gear we'd brought and kept walking. Hours later we arrived in Grasmere, totally drenched, but fine otherwise. It didn't matter that we were wet—we had clean, dry clothes in our backpacks and could change as soon as we got to the bed and breakfast where we'd reserved a room.

But the backpacks had not protected the contents against the heavy rain and everything inside was wet. Luckily, the kind lady who ran the bed and breakfast put all our clothes in her dryer and by the time we'd had our baths there were clothes to wear. Since then, we always pack our clothing into plastic bags. Anything like a strong garbage bag is fine for the purpose. If it's clear plastic, so much the better—you will know what's inside without having to open each bag.

I do the same for anything I carry with me that may suffer from rain: passport, maps, notes, money. There are plenty of good household plastic bags available—with ties or ziplocks—of every conceivable size to make packing things easy.

Again, if you're walking in clear, dry weather and know you can rely on that, packing into plastic bags isn't necessary. But because the mountains are particularly prone to unexpected weather, wise practice is to protect your clothing. Walking in the rain isn't nearly as problematic, as you'll have on protective clothing and should remain relatively dry inside. In fact, you may well enjoy the experience, as long as it doesn't happen every day.

Drugstore and Medical Supplies

I'm going to mention a lot of things to take along in this section, but nothing that is big or heavy. You may never actually need a given item, but it's better to have brought it than wish you had.

For Your Feet

There are wonderful foam cushions and pads for every part of your foot, even places where you didn't know you could have a problem. Some of these could be useful after you have been walking for an hour or two, especially if your new boots aren't properly worn in. You may suddenly find that the shoe is pressing on a toe or on the side of your foot, that a blister is starting to form or that your have discomfort as you walk uphill or downhill. It's for this reason that you have to go to a well-supplied drugstore and look over all their foot bandages, padded strips, corn pads, thumb caps, and whatever else is available. Buy a good selection and take them with you, hoping that you'll never break open a package. Because some of the products have to be cut to size, bring a small pair of scissors, points well protected, as well. (Perhaps your folding knife includes scissors.)

The moment you feel discomfort, stop walking, find a place to sit, and tend to your foot. Never try to be a martyr when you feel pain in your feet. Never neglect to put a bandage on a tender spot. The rule is that your feet will never feel better if you ignore the pain and keep walking. They will only become worse. Once you have taken care of your foot, go on with your walk. If there's more trouble later, add another bandage. If you deal with the problem immediately, it shouldn't interfere with the rest of your day.

And Your Legs

It may never happen—and perhaps this will be insurance against it—but it's a good idea to pack an ace-bandage with your other supplies. In case someone twists an ankle this could be important in facilitating her return to base camp.

Medication

If you have any medication that has to be taken regularly during the course of the day, remember to take it with you. Don't leave it until you get home in the evening and, certainly, never take a double dose because you forgot to take your medicine on the walk.

If you tend to get headaches, and take aspirin or anything similar, make sure that they come with you as well. In fact, bringing along a pain reliever is a good idea, just in case of unforeseen injury.

In case of long walks that will take you far from "civilization" it's a good idea to pack in an antihistamine (the non-sedating kind) in case you get problematic bites or you have an allergic reaction to something.

Other Drugstore Items

Besides the products designed specifically for feet, you should bring along ordinary bandages or sterile pads and adhesive, in case someone falls or gets scratched. And for this purpose, too, bring along a tube of first aid cream. We have almost never needed these, but we prefer to have them with us.

For walks in sunny weather, sunscreen is a must. Check out what kind of protection you need for your skin and bring along a container. To save yourself the trouble, put on some before you leave home on your walk, if it seems likely that you'll be out in the sun soon.

Something else that we have seldom needed but would prefer to have "just in case" is repellant against mosquitoes, black flies, or whatever local biting insects are there. You can walk for days or even weeks without encountering mosquitoes, but if there's a risk, be prepared. We have had very rare occasions when we needed repellant, but those episodes were so memorable that they are indelibly etched in our family history. In fact, if you are going to an area that is new to you, it is worth asking about such insects, either before you leave or when you are there and can talk to the locals.

It follows that if you don't bring along a repellant, or if it isn't effective, you'll have to have an itch reliever. This could be in the form of lotion or antihistamine tablets.

After an exquisite late afternoon walk on Mount Desert Island off the coast of Maine, my husband and older daughter encountered, or rather were discovered by, a swarm of mosquitoes, well known in New England in the late spring. Luckily for me and my younger daughter the mosquitoes centered their attention on the two of them and caused a very dramatic dash for the car, leaving us to make our way in a more leisurely fashion. Almost as awful was the time we were attacked by swarms of black flies in New Hampshire. (This is a seasonal and localized problem that may not affect you when you plan your hiking.)

And then there was the encounter in the Scottish Highlands, when my husband and I had clambered halfway up a mountain covered in heather. We suddenly engaged the attention of something small and potent, many of them, so that in the end we threw all caution to the winds and dashed down the mountain by a very direct descent. Later that afternoon we asked about the insects that had stung us and someone with a dry sense of humor in the local drugstore asked if it was at all possible that we could have come up against some midges. Imagine! We had indeed. And although the proprietor seemed skeptical that his area could be guilty of having anything so inhospitable, on the way out I noticed, prominently placed by the cash register, a large bowl filled with containers of anti-midge spray for sale.

Bring along some tissues in a packet and put them into a side pocket of your backpack or into your own pocket for easy access. You will also want to bring along a long strip of toilet paper in a small plastic bag also kept in an accessible place.

Needless to say, if it's one of those days, don't forget tampons or sanitary napkins, enough for a whole day. You won't be able to buy them

INSECT BITES:

If you are bitten and the bite becomes red, swollen, or pussy, or if red streaks run up your arm from the area of the bite, these could be signs of infection.

SUGGESTION:

If you only plan to use your backpack for hiking and will be storing it the rest of the time, leave certain basic items in it permanently to save yourself the trouble of organizing them each time you take a walk. For example, keep your supply of bandages, foot pads, first-aid cream, tissues, toilet paper, scissors, Swiss knife and a compass in your pack, ready for use whenever you are in the mood to hike.

along the way, so even if you think there's only a slight chance of needing one, bring it.

Food and Drink

The most important thing of all is water. You must bring enough water with you for the entire day's walking. It doesn't matter if it's tap water or bottled, bring along at least a quart and more if you can manage it. If it's a hot day and you don't think you'll be passing any place where drinks can be bought, bring two bottles.

Bottles for carrying water can be purchased in any outdoors store, in either plastic or metal. Get bottles that can fit into the outside pocket of you backpack. Be sure to fill them before leaving for your walk. If your first stop is to take off the warm outer garments, your second pause will be to have a drink. It's important and generally accepted today that people should have plenty to drink in hot weather or if they are expending a lot of energy. (Years ago people were discouraged from drinking during heavy exercise, but the commonly held view today is that it is important to avoid dehydration.) So don't deprive yourself of water. Figure on pausing to drink every twenty minutes or half hour in warm weather and try to combine that with other needs—taking off a piece of clothing, adjusting your backpack, checking the map, taking pictures. But if you stop for a drink when it's chilly, don't stand around too long. In general, you should plan on your long break when you stop for lunch.

Lunch

It's great fun to take lunch with you, even if it's not always necessary. The situation varies from location to location. In the Swiss Alps, for instance, you can usually count on getting to a pleasant restaurant after a few hours' walk. In the Rockies, however, if you don't carry your lunch with you, you'll go hungry.

If you are on vacation and staying in a hotel, you will be able to ask them to prepare a packed lunch for you. These can often be quite glorious but they may be more than you want to eat and they can be pretty bulky to stuff into a backpack. They can also be quite expensive. We tend to pick up our own food for lunch so it ends up cheaper, very fresh, just what we want, and fun to do, especially if you like food shopping in new places. There's something refreshing about going into a local bakery to pick up freshly-baked rolls and some cheese sliced to order from the local grocery store, whether you're in the United States or abroad.

Take things for lunch that are easy to pack in, don't get crushed easily, travel well. With our rolls, we tend to take along cheese, which fulfills all these qualifications. We don't make sandwiches in advance, but cut up the rolls and cheese high up in the mountains. So something else for the list of things to be packed in is a knife. Bring a Swiss-type knife that closes safely and has a couple of blades and any other gadget you may need, but nothing too big or heavy.

You'll also want some fruit. Even if you'd prefer a peach, take an apple or some other very firm fruit. We sometimes take oranges because they're so refreshing, though the down side is that they can be messy.

And, perhaps, a dessert: cookies, a bar of chocolate. You'll walk it off after lunch. (But if you are really doing the walking as part of an overall diet/health regime, skip that.)

You may also want to bring a thermos with hot tea or coffee. Many climbers like to have a hot drink when they stop for their break, especially as the natural place for lunch is someplace quite high up and often chilly.

Snacks

Bring along some snacks to eat any time during the day that you need some energy food. Lots of things can be recommended in this category:

Dried fruit

Nuts

Hard candies

Mints (very popular in the Lake District where there's something called Kendal mint cake)

Extra fresh fruit

Any favorite snack food

Hiking Accessories and Equipment

Everything else falls into this category. There are a number of things to bring along to make your hike safer and easier. Some of the items are necessary and others are optional.

Maps

You should never take a walk in the mountains without a map. As you saw in the map chapter, while it is true that in some areas the paths are extremely well marked, you still want to have a map.

If you ordinarily wear **reading glasses**, take them (or a magnifying glass) along for looking at the fine print on the map. You don't want to be caught out there with a map and no way to read it.

You will also want to take a **map case**. A decent map case can be bought for a small amount of money. When it starts to rain and you have to take out your map, it will be much more readable if it's protected under plastic. The case often comes with cord, so that you can wear it around you neck. In that situation you'll want to put the map in upside down, folded to the specific section you're in, so that you can read it without taking it off. If you don't feel comfortable wearing it, place it in the upper flap of your backpack, if the top has a zippered compartment for maps. Many of them do. Otherwise, tuck it into an available outside pocket.

Compass

Here again, you may or may not actually need one, but a cheap compass that locates the north accurately can be a godsend sometimes. If you are just starting out in mountain walking and don't feel comfortable finding your way by compass, then choose a mountain area where it's not necessary. But there are many beautiful and safe places for mountain walking where you will be happier with a compass, at least on your second or third try at the sport.

We were once caught in heavy fog on a mountain in Cumbria where we could barely see our own feet. Using the compass was our only way of making sure that we got on a path that would lead us down into the right valley.

Flashlight

You should never need this. Always arrange your walks so that you get back home in daylight. But if, for some reason, you find yourself walking in the dark on a mountain path, you'll definitely be glad you brought a flashlight. If you go to the trouble of bringing one, make sure that the batteries are fresh. Instead of bringing a large heavy flashlight, you might prefer one of the good slim styles that have a light that can be adjusted to give a broad beam on the path or a thin one.

Whistle

It's such a small item, just throw it into an outside pocket. A whistle is recommended if you're caught in the fog. Walking on the Island of Skye once we ended up in very thick fog. Although a whole group of us (including a number of children) were walking single file we could barely see each other and the whistles did actually help.

Walking Stick

While this is optional, many walkers, young and old, find that using a walking stick increases their stability and enjoyment when walking on rough or slippery terrain. It may enable you to cross a difficult patch more quickly or without concern. In the Himalayas I have often picked up a good length of bamboo to serve as a walking stick and enjoyed it. In fact, today hikers frequently opt for two, carrying one in each hand for better balance. They're often sold in sporting goods stores in pairs and are referred to as trekking poles, though you should be able to buy a single one if you feel you'd rather keep one hand free.

A second use for trekking poles is aerobic: they provide additional upper-body exercise in the way that the use of ski poles does in cross-country skiing. While you can use a makeshift stick (or ski poles), the advantage of the one made specifically for this function is that it comes in a compact size that can be extended according to your height. When you're not using it, it is short enough to be carried comfortably, attached to your backpack.

Altimeter

This is optional, but adds something to a long walk. There are other ways to know how high you are: you can, for example, just look at the map and figure out the altitude from the contours. But an altimeter is useful if you don't know exactly where you are or have no landmarks to judge by. While it is an enjoyable accessory, be forewarned that an altimeter can be expensive and is not strictly necessary.

GPS
Use of a global positioning system device is also optional (and expensive). My guess is that they will come in at lower prices once they become a hot-selling item. It's certainly not necessary for the average mountain walk in the Rockies, the White Mountains, the Alps, or any other initial walking you may do.

Other Equipment
There are a few other things that you might want to have with you on a day's walking. You may think of others in this category.

Watch
I haven't mentioned a watch on the assumption that most people wear one anyway. But if you don't wear a wristwatch religiously, do remember to take it in the mountains. It's important to know the time, how long it has taken to get to where you're going, and when the sun is due to set. If you find that the first part of your walk has taken far longer than you expected, you may want to turn around and head back, even if you haven't reached your destination. The last thing that you want is to find yourself high up in the mountains when the sun is about to set.

Camera
This is optional, but if you ever take pictures, this is the time to have a camera with you. Mountains are wonderfully photogenic (though difficult to do justice on film) and you may find yourself taking photographs of the same mountain from different angles, at different times of the day or with a variety of clouds in the background. And, of course, make sure to bring enough film with you. A few rolls can be dropped into a plastic bag and put into an outside pocket of your backpack. When you change rolls, you can put the used film back in. Because many people don't recognize mountains easily (they don't all have the shape of the Matterhorn!) you may want to have a few scraps of paper and a pencil in with the film so that you can note the names of the mountains on the roll that you've just taken and slip them into the case. It will be useful

when you're putting together an album later. If you've been using your map well you'll be able to identify which mountain you've been photographing.

Cellular Phone

Although this is not necessary—and we ourselves have never used one in the mountains—you might feel more comfortable taking a cellular phone, especially if you are used to carrying one around with you. (This would only be possible in areas that can accommodate the transmission of calls and should be checked out in advance.)

My advice would be to use the cellular phone, though, only in case of necessity and not for communicating with friends. The beauty of a mountain vacation is that you can get away from it all and enjoy the wonders of nature and the company of whomever you're with. Chatting on the phone as you climb up toward a towering peak somehow doesn't fit the bill!

These are the basic items to take along. They may seem to be a lot, but it's really only extra clothing, some bandages, sun protection, food and drink. Here's a checklist so that you can be sure you have everything you need for your first day's walk.

Checklist for Backpack

Clothing
- ✓ Warm sweater
- ✓ Sweatshirt
- ✓ Raingear
- ✓ Hat
- ✓ Warm cap
- ✓ Gloves
- ✓ Scarf
- ✓ Dry socks
- ✓ Plastic bags

Drugstore items
- ✓ Foot supplies
- ✓ Bandages

- ✓ Scissors
- ✓ First-aid cream
- ✓ Ace bandage
- ✓ Sunscreen
- ✓ Mosquito repellant and itch reliever (optional)
- ✓ Medicine (optional)
- ✓ Tampons/sanitary napkins (if necessary)

Food
- ✓ Water
- ✓ Lunch
- ✓ Fruit
- ✓ Snacks

Hiking Accessories
- ✓ Maps
- ✓ Map case
- ✓ Compass
- ✓ Swiss knife
- ✓ Flashlight
- ✓ Whistle
- ✓ Watch
- ✓ Camera (optional)
- ✓ Film (optional)
- ✓ Sunglasses
- ✓ Altimeter (optional)
- ✓ GPS (optional)
- ✓ Cellular phone (optional)

My own backpack, loaded with all the clothing, including anorak, full water bottle, lunch, everything, weighs between 11 and 12 pounds. Add more for the camera. This is an acceptable weight for a day's walk and, if the pack is adjusted well, it should be easy to carry.

The Mountains: A Family Affair

During a week's vacation in Courmayeur in the Italian Alps one summer, my husband came down with a bad cold. The weather was beautiful, the mountains beckoned, and I hated to think of hanging around the hotel all day with our fourteen-month-old daughter. So after breakfast, I put Leora into the papoose, slipped it on my back, took along a little food and a diaper and set out on a walk by myself. Well, not really by myself, because Leora sat happily on my back, looking over my shoulder, and enjoying the rhythm of my walking until she fell asleep. The result: I had a good four hours to enjoy the mountains and got back in time for a late lunch with a husband who was feeling much better.

This may sound overly simple and ideal, but if you have a baby who loves a papoose—as my first daughter did—then walking in the mountains with her can be not only painless but fun.

A mountain vacation can be a wonderful experience to be enjoyed by the family. The problems you may encounter and the pleasures that can be derived vary with the age of your child.

Let me start with babies.

Mountains and Babies

The reason that you take a baby to the mountains is because you want to be there and you don't want to leave your baby behind. This is a different kind of rationale from deciding to take children and teenagers to the mountains, where you are also considering what they would like. So let's start out by agreeing that when you take your baby on a trip of this kind—even for a day in the mountains not far from home—it's because you really don't want to feel that you're being cut off from this kind of sport just because you're a young (or perhaps not so young!) mother.

What Do I Do with the Baby?

The easiest way to handle the problem of the baby is just to take him with you on your walk. This is especially convenient if you are still breast-feeding.

CARRIERS

You are limited in the kind of carrier you can use if your baby is under six months old. Don't be fooled into thinking that because the baby seems comfortable propped up in a sitting position that it is all right to carry him that way. You can cause serious damage if you force a sitting position too early. The main concern here is head control. When the baby has adequate head control—it doesn't just bob back and forth—he can be carried in a papoose on the back. So if your baby is eight months old and still not sitting on his own but holds his head steadily, he can be carried in a papoose anyway. But placing a baby in a papoose before he has good head control could cause the breakage of very small blood vessels in the brain and minor hemorrhages.

A young baby can be carried in a front pack or in a sling in the front or on the side. With this setup you could even carry a backpack at the same time, although it's clearly better if you carry one load and someone else carries the other. The front-worn carrier for smaller babies holds the infant so that he is nestled up against your chest. Such a carrier is pretty comfortable for holding a very little baby, but once the baby is heavier there is a real strain on your back, which can make long-distance walking uncomfortable.

You may find that the sling is more comfortable over a long walk, though neither of these options is ideal. But you don't have a perfect solution when your baby is small. When the baby is a couple of months old, you can adjust the sling to rest partly on the hip, which helps distribute the baby's weight better. This is an important consideration.

I strongly suggest that you hunt for the right carrier for a young baby well before you plan to go climbing. After you've bought the carrier, use it, making sure not only that you can take long walks with it comfortably but also that the baby is happy in it. You may have to acclimatize him to being carried in this way.

Qian Luo

You should check with your pediatrician about the advisability of *any carrier for an infant to make sure that it is suitable for his age and stage of development.*

Once your baby has adequate head control—that is, from the age of six months old or so—you can use a papoose, which is by far the most comfortable arrangement for hiking or mountain walking. It is suitable not only for babies, but for toddlers as well. Depending upon your child's size and preference, you will find the papoose an option until about age three. In the papoose, the baby or toddler usually sits facing forward (although models vary) partially protected from wind and cold by the back of his parent. Some papooses even have little awnings to keep the sun from beating down on the baby's head hour after hour. While the baby is awake he can see all around him from a fine vantage point and when he falls asleep he can find a good position without getting cramped. The papoose is an ideal carrier.

The success of the papoose is not so surprising. In traditional societies women have carried their babies constantly, usually on the back. Indeed, today there is a movement to encourage modern parents to continue this practice of keeping the baby in close bodily contact all the time in order to increase the infant's sense of well being.

You may notice when you hike with your baby on your back that the reassuring rhythm of your walking and the soothing position against your back induce a calmer mood in your child. You may also find that your child sleeps much more when you're in the mountains—either in the papoose or at night in bed. The exposure to fresh air and the cooler temperatures often induces sleep. Don't worry about it: enjoy it! (You may find that you will also sleep longer and better in the mountains.)

"In the infant kept in constant contact with the body of a caretaker, his energy field becomes one with hers and excess energy can be discharged for both of them by her activities alone. The infant can remain relaxed, free of accumulating tension, as his extra energy flows into hers."

—*Jean Liedloff,*
The Continuum Concept

There are disadvantages with the papoose, though. For example, as the baby is behind you, you really can't see what's happening to him. You also cannot carry anything else on your back once the papoose is there (though some papooses have a small carrier compartment at the bottom). I therefore strongly advise that if you are planning to take your baby to the mountains you go with someone else. If your partner, for example, is carrying the baby, you can be the one to carry the backpack (which may well be lighter). You will also be able to see how the baby is doing, whether he has fallen asleep, has the sun in his eyes, or is in an awkward position.

Dressing for the Mountains

You will have to dress the baby differently from the way you dress yourself. After all, you are walking, using energy, keeping warm through activity. The baby is just sitting. While it is true that some warmth and protection are coming from the parent's body, it is still necessary to dress the baby for the cooler air of the mountain—and the higher you go the colder it will become. So even if you are just walking in a t-shirt while you climb, if the air is cool your baby will need a jacket, mittens, and a cap. Alternatively, the baby will need a sun hat as protection in bright weather.

Besides a hat, the baby will need other protection from the sun. Doctors do not recommend putting sunscreen on babies under one year of age, not because it's bad for them but for fear that it will give the mother a false sense of security. Instead, make sure your baby is well covered, even in hot weather, with a sun hat, long sleeves (it can be light material) and long pants, as the best safeguard.

How Long Can We Take the Baby in the Papoose?

The amount of time a child will stay in a papoose is an individual question and the answer depends very much on his nature. If your baby is comfortable and happy, you can go out for hours. If he falls asleep, he should also be fine for a long period of time. But at some point you will stop for a break, either to picnic or to eat in a mountain restaurant. This will give the baby or toddler a chance to be taken out of the papoose and move around.

With a toddler, you may also succeed in taking him out of the papoose and encouraging him to do some of the walking himself. This sometimes works very well, but it may backfire. On a recent visit in the Swiss Alps we tried to convince our toddler grandson to come out of the papoose and do some walking on his own, but he was very comfortable perched up in his nest and resisted every effort to get him out. It was only when we got up to a very snowy area that he suddenly insisted upon walking. But at this point we were on a slippery path with a sizable drop on one side. This did not concern him. He wanted out. Luckily, I managed to convince Ariel to hold my hand the whole time he was walking. He loved it, but when he tired, I was delighted to put him in his papoose again, on his father's back.

Food

Because you cannot always be sure to find just what your baby or toddler likes to eat, you should bring a certain amount of food for him. You don't want to end up in a situation where he is hungry and you can't find anything suitable in the mountain restaurant you've just reached. On many mountain walks, you have to bring food along not just for your child but for your own lunch needs anyway. And don't forget the baby's drink. If you're a nursing mother, you can usually find a convenient off-path spot to sit down and feed the baby. Otherwise, pack in a bottle!

Altitude

On another day during my trip to Courmayeur, when my daughter was an infant, I took her on the local chair lift system to the highest station. It was a long trip, starting with a cable car and then a series of chair lifts. The baby was fine and seemed to be enjoying herself until we got to the last stop high up on a snowy mountain. At this point she started crying and I tried to figure out what was wrong with her. Was there a pin sticking in her? Was she suddenly hungry? But there was no open safety pin and she didn't want a banana or a drink. She just kept crying. I turned around and took the chair lift one stop down to a lower altitude and the crying stopped. She was fine.

Babies can be more sensitive to high altitude than adults are. Their ears often react to air pressure. You've probably seen this phenomenon with babies on an airplane, even though the cabin is pressurized. So you have to use your judgment in taking your baby or toddler up very high. If you are gradually walking up, there is less of a chance that your child will suffer a bad reaction to the height. But if you are going up rapidly in a cable car or chair lift don't go too high too fast. I would be careful above 8,000 feet.

Where Not to Take Your Baby

I would not advise any kind of exotic mountain trip with a baby or toddler where you are not sure of the quality of the water supply or the health system. Don't go to a country where you have been warned that you should be careful with the food or should avoid raw fruits and vegetables. It's just not worth it. Do that kind of trip before you've got young children or when you can safely leave them behind (or when they're not at home with you anyway!). There are so many wonderful mountain regions where you can feel safe with your baby or toddler that you should be satisfied with enjoying them in the mean time.

CHECKLIST OF WHAT TO BRING ON A WALK FOR A BABY OR TODDLER

- ✓ Extra diapers. (You won't find any to buy along the way.)
- ✓ Wet wipes in a plastic container.
- ✓ Plastic bag. (To carry dirty diapers back down.)
- ✓ Insect repellant usable for babies. (You're outdoors all day: there could be bugs, depending on the season.)
- ✓ Baby's food.
- ✓ A spoon for feeding the baby.
- ✓ Snack food for baby.
- ✓ Plenty to drink.
- ✓ Change of clothes. (You don't want him to remain wet if there's a mishap.)
- ✓ Rainproof gear. (The papoose won't protect a child from rain.)
- ✓ Thermos. (If your toddler likes warm soup in cool weather—or if you have to keep something cold.)
- ✓ Sunscreen suitable for toddlers. (Even if the mountain air is cool, there can be plenty of sun.)
- ✓ Extra sweater or jacket (in case the weather turns cold).
- ✓ Cap and mittens (if he's not already wearing them).
- ✓ Sun hat.
- ✓ Any blanket or pacifier that the baby is attached to and can't do without for the day.

Young Children

Potentially the most difficult time to take your child to the mountains is between the toddler stage—when you can still carry him comfortably on your back or shoulders—and the age when he is able to walk a considerable distance on his own. The point at which he becomes a walker varies with the child. It could be as young as four or as old as six or seven. I know a family whose three-year-old walks with them for hours.

When our younger daughter, Rachel, was four years old, we were in the French Alps for a short time, staying in Chamonix. It was autumn, a beautiful (though unreliable) season in the mountains. Rachel was just entering the stage of being a sturdy little walker and we decided to give her a chance to prove herself. We offered a reward of a little backpack of her own if she could complete a whole walk one day. The route we chose was in the easy category for an adult: a couple of hours of walking a thousand feet up the mountain and down again. She made a concerted effort, did it successfully and received her prize. (Eight-year-old Leora, observing it all, thought her little sister was crazy to give up sitting on Daddy's shoulders at least part of the time just to get to carry things on her back!)

Technically, you can carry a child up a mountain path as long as he's not too heavy. But once your child weighs thirty-five pounds or more that's quite a load. After that you have to depend on the ability of the child himself to do the walking.

If you have a child at this stage and you definitely want to have a mountain vacation I suggest a few variations:

Spelling Each Other Off
Why not organize a trip together with friends? You and your walking companions can take turns climbing while someone stays down below in the village with the child. If you are travelling with other couples, and there are a few children, you should organize your time fairly so that every couple or group gets a chance to enjoy the hiking while someone else is looking after the children. If you can possibly manage it, though, *you should try to do some climbing together with your child,*

whether he's walking or being carried, and not just leave him down below.
Give him a taste of the mountains: it's never too early. Another technique
if you're with a group of friends is that you can all start out together
and then let someone take the kids back down early while the others
keep going.

Grandparents

If you'd like an opportunity to travel with your parents or in-laws, this
could be the perfect opportunity. If the grandparents are still youthful
and active they'll love the opportunity to walk in the mountains as
much as you do.

Active grandparents can be harnessed the same way other travelling
companions are: take turns with them so that you do the walking in the
morning and then come down, relieve them of the child care, and let them
do the walking in the afternoon and vice versa. If they really don't want
to do any walking—and I hope that's not the case—they can simply enjoy
the ambience of a mountain village, breathe in the wholesome air, marvel
at the views, do some driving around the area and look after their grand-
child for a portion of the day while you have an active vacation.

If you do plan to go with the older generation, urge them to get into
shape, at least by doing some walking at home before they meet you.
The mountains can be enjoyed by every age and by all people in basi-
cally good health. Switzerland is full of older people who have maintained their health and continue to take pleasure in the mountains well
into their seventies and eighties. The grandparents will enjoy their
vacation with you if the babysitting is not overdone and they have an
opportunity to do their own walking as well. Today, with so many people over fifty doing aerobic walking and exercises, you may find that
your parents are in better shape than you are.

Special Tips

***   USE A STROLLER WHEN POSSIBLE. As long as your child can still
fit in a stroller, use it for any paths that can take one. Many mountain
paths are smooth enough and well graded for use of a stroller, though it
takes a lot of energy.

***   USE ANY MEANS OF TRANSPORTATION AVAILABLE TO GET UP HIGHER.
As your child's energy is limited, try using the chair lifts, cable cars, and

other transportation available to get you up to a better starting point to begin walking with your small child. The ride in itself is fun and it will enable you to get to higher ground and better vistas quickly. Keep in mind that there should not be too high an altitude change at once, however.

*** BRIBERY. It's an ugly word, but you can get kids going if they know there'll be a reward—beyond a feeling of accomplishment—if they succeed. I'm not suggesting paying kids by the mile or by the height climbed. That would be defeating the idea of instilling a love for the mountains in your family. But there are all kinds of ways that every parent knows of encouraging children to do things they're wary of but will like if they actually do them.

Babysitters

In many places you can find babysitters. You may want one in the daytime for an opportunity to go off on your own, unencumbered. You could well need a babysitter in the evening if you want to go out to dinner alone.

If you are staying in a hotel, they can often provide you with a sitter. In some mountain resorts, for example in Swiss villages, you can contact the local municipal tourist office for a list of available sitters, though you'll want to make sure that the person you select can speak English to your child.

If you just need a sitter for a couple of hours in the evening, you can give the sitter the phone number of your restaurant and ask to be called if there's trouble. Leaving a child during the day and for a longer period can be more problematic. Before doing this, make sure that the sitter and your child get along and that you are satisfied about the care he will receive. Once you're out walking there's no way to get in touch with you, short of a cell phone that may not operate in mountainous terrain. Satellite phones are an option, but a very expensive one at this point.

Where to Stay

Travelling with babies and young children can sometimes be easier if you're not in a hotel room. In many places, you can rent an apartment or chalet-type house. In Grand Teton National Park or Rocky Mountain National Park, for example, you can get lovely wooden bungalows that look rustic on the outside but are very comfortable and modern inside.

In Swiss villages, it is easy to rent an apartment or chalet and it works out to be much cheaper than hotel rooms. You also have more room to move around in, an important consideration with children of any age. The apartment gives you the added convenience of having your own little kitchen (well equipped), which is often essential when you're feeding a small child. Once you have a refrigerator you can store whatever you need. Heating up food is also easier. So consider this option when you're deciding on a vacation spot.

Catering to the Interests of Young Children

Even at the more difficult age of three to six, children can enjoy various aspects of the mountains. Some of these points of interests will also appeal to older kids and adults of all ages.

***   SPECIAL ACTIVITIES FOR YOUNG CHILDREN. In some mountain resorts you'll find a playground in the village or a swimming pool or miniature golf.

***   ENJOYING WILDLIFE. Many areas, including some of the national parks, abound in wild animals, from chipmunks and squirrels to bears, elk, and moose. Selecting this kind of mountain range will add an extra component of interest for children.

***   FARMS AND FARM ANIMALS. In other places serious farming and animal husbandry are carried out right in the mountains. Children— and everyone else—love the Swiss cows high up in the Alps with the huge bells around their necks clanging away. There are also sheep there (and elsewhere) and goats. Coming upon flocks, stopping to look at them, watching them graze, seeing their lambs or calves is an education in itself for children.

***   ZOOS. In some mountain resorts there are interesting zoos exhibiting animals and birds whose natural habitat is the mountains. I took Rachel to one up in the Mont Blanc area in France and we spent a long time while she stared at an owl and the owl stared back until I became so cold I insisted on going inside.

***   CHILD-SIZE EXPEDITIONS. There are often special sights that are interesting for all ages and require little expenditure of real energy so that the smaller child can manage it without help. Various areas offer caves, caverns, waterfalls, ice formations, and other natural wonders that make good side trips.

Walking with School-Age Children

In a way, children from six to twelve or thirteen are the easiest ones to take to the mountains. They still enjoy travelling with their parents. They like activity and are strong enough to be able to walk real distances. Once children are walking well they can outdo their parents. My daughters used to stride ahead and reach our destination well ahead of me. Granted, they might also tire faster—truly a tortoise-and-hare situation—but we were able to enjoy major walks with them from the time they reached elementary-school age. Many children take to the mountains like ducks to water.

> Scientists note a significant increase in obesity in children. This can lead to serious health problems.
> *"Lack of physical activity contributes to the problem. Fewer than half of American schoolchildren participate in daily physical education. Television, video games and computers add to the problems of sedentary living."*
> —Washington Post, *October 1998*

You may have a child who is awkward or doesn't see himself as "athletic." Perhaps he's overweight, has grown faster than his peers and feels uncomfortable with his height, feels clumsy or tends toward the sedentary. He may be good in one area—at school—but not in another—physical skills. Such a child, or one who is timid or anxious, can gain confidence in walking, especially when he sees that he can actually manage the route and keep up with the family. He will have a real sense of accomplishment if he is able to meet the challenge. This can give a tremendous boost to the child's self-confidence.

Make sure that you bring along plenty to eat and

NOTE:

Don't treat the mountains as an obstacle course. Start out gradually and build up the amount you do day after day. Don't push too hard in the beginning. If you've had a fairly tough day of walking, then try to take it easy the next day. Remember, the whole family is supposed to be having a good time—and you will if you plan your walks well.

drink and stop frequently enough for your child to drink enough along the way. It is important to avoid dehydration. For an adult as well as for a child, there is a simple way to check: the color of urine—except in the morning when it is more yellow—should be pale. If it is too concentrated or dark in color, then the person must drink a lot more.

Teenagers on the Trail

It can be hard to find vacation activities that your entire family—including teenagers—will enjoy together. Walking in the mountains can be an ideal solution.

Mountaineering can provide a far more successful vacation than visiting a city as a family, seeing museums and public buildings, especially if your teenagers have limited patience for paintings, architecture or medieval armor. Physical activity puts you all on an equal level and can even let the kids excel at times. It can also serve as an equalizer among siblings. Walking together in the mountains can cement family relationships and give you something to reminisce about together later.

First, it breeds a sense of well being and a feeling of accomplishment. You can all see yourselves improving your skills and trying more difficult or lengthier walks as the days go by.

Second, there is an element of adventure in mountain walking which appeals to most teenagers. They will not only enjoy the sense of discovery in climbing, but they will also have something to tell their friends about when they get home. Even getting caught in the rain is an adventure when you're on a mountain path.

Third, it is something that everybody can do at his own speed. You don't necessarily all have to walk together, as long as you meet up every once in a while along the path. (It may work better if one adult member of the group moves on at a faster pace with the older kids and someone else brings up the rear with the slower walkers.) We were once caught in heavy rain in the Alps, so my husband moved on quickly with two-year-old Rachel on his shoulders and me walking at six-year-old Leora's speed. By the time we arrived, quite wet, at the shelter we were heading for, hot soup was on the table and a change of clothes already out of the backpack.

It may be that your teenagers will be delighted at the idea of a family vacation in the mountains. If they seem less enthusiastic or need encouragement, here are some suggestions:

Getting the Most out of the Mountains with Teenagers in the Family
Many of these suggestions can be useful for younger children as well.

***   PHOTOGRAPHY. If you feel that the mountain walking itself won't be sufficiently attractive for your teenager (or younger child), why not make it into a photographic expedition? Walking in the mountains is challenging and so is photographing them. Photography will add another interesting component to the trip and your child will end up with an impressive album as a result. Your child should have her own camera or sole use of one on the trip. This may be an occasion for upgrading equipment, acquiring filters, learning more about photography.

***   FLOWERS, BIRDS. Observing and cataloging botany and birds is an enjoyable activity for many people young or old. Bring along books (or buy them in the area) for identifying the wildflowers that you'll see along the way or the various birds that are flying in the mountains. Because of the very nature of mountains, they host a wide variety of plants and trees that may not be seen in the plains.

***   MAP READING. It's fun to work out a route on a map. Before you even start, you and the kids can sit down with a map and plot out your walk. Then use the map as you go along, choosing the right path at each intersection. This is an important skill to have and your teenager can get a much clearer view of the map when it is applied to a real walk. She can learn how to work out contours, how to judge distance and height. She'll have input. It's also fun.

***   BRING BINOCULARS. One of the exciting aspects of being in the mountains is the endless variety of spectacular views. Bring along binoculars. You'll be able to get close-up views of the birds or wildlife that abound in some of the mountain areas. You can catch sight of distant houses, lakes, ,and other landmarks marked on a detailed area map. This will help the kids' map reading and maintain interest in the progress of the walk. As with many of the suggestions in this list, this is something that adults will fully enjoy too, not just the kids.

*** BOOKS ON THE MOUNTAINS AND MOUNTAINEERING. There are wonderful books on mountains, often sumptuously illustrated. They make good vacation reading.

*** USING MOUNTAINEERING AIDS. Even if you don't necessarily need them, it will be fun for the family to make use of mountaineering aids on your walk. Get a compass. It doesn't have to be an expensive one, just anything that will show North. Let the kids orient themselves with it and work out the route using the points of the compass. It's always interesting on a climb to have an altimeter and a pedometer. The cost is higher than for a compass, but if you can manage it, they're exciting. With all these aids, you'll be able to work out exactly where you are, how high you've climbed, how much further you have to go up. It may well add to the appeal of longer walks.

*** ABSEILING OR MOUNTAINEERING LESSONS. As your children start to enjoy their walking in the mountains, some of them may want to branch out and learn climbing techniques. In many mountain resorts there are qualified teachers for young and old who give classes in the use of ropes in rock climbing. Even though this is not what you are planning to do in the mountains, your children could find it a very pleasant and exciting new skill. And you may decide to join them.

*** BRING ALONG A FRIEND. If you plan to be taking just one child with you, it is possible that he will balk at being alone with adults. He could well see this as "boring." I think that all parents face this problem at some point, especially when the youngest child in the family suddenly finds himself on his own because his older brother or sister isn't coming on vacation with the family this year. You should consider having your child bring along a friend to share the fun. This is often a good solution when a child starts grumbling about yet another vacation with his parents.

*** TRY SKIING FOR A CHANGE. One summer we organized a three-week stay in Zermatt in the Swiss Alps. It's a village with innumerable possibilities for walks, truly a wonderful place for a mountain vacation. But we hadn't taken our children into account sufficiently. They started to get the feeling that they were just going up a mountain and then down again, and never "getting anywhere." After the first week or ten days they started to complain that they'd had enough. Because Zermatt has year-long snow on the Klein Matterhorn, ten thousand feet up, there is good summer skiing. So we signed up the girls (then ten and fourteen) for skiing lessons and they started going up to the ski area early every morning for lessons. They loved it. We kept up our walking and they learned to ski—well, Rachel spent much of her time falling off the T-bar, but at least she mastered that and some down-hill skills during the next week. We all ended up very happy.

*** SELECT A MOUNTAIN RESORT WITH VARIED ACTIVITIES. Many mountain resorts offer a variety of extra activities. Skiing is only available in very special locations that enjoy the high altitude and summer snow. But in many other regions you can find boating, white water rafting, tennis, ping pong, horseback riding, swimming and other sports that young and old would enjoy either during the off-hours from walking or on a day off from hiking. Even if there's no suitable lake or coast in the area, a local hotel may have an indoor swimming pool. Investigate the activities available if you want to make sure that there's more to do than walking when you take your family to the mountains.

*** BACKPACKING. For the child from eleven or twelve on the prospect of backpacking can be very attractive. It offers a different level of adventure and enjoyment because you end up walking to constantly new destinations and are sleeping in a different place every night. Everything you need is carried on your back: change of clothes, pajamas, sneakers for the evening. I would suggest starting with a two-day backpacking trip where you'll just have one overnight stay en route. This will cut down on the amount that has to be carried on each back and will offer a less pressured introduction to a new sport. We did our first backpacking with our kids when our younger daughter was twelve. The kids found it very exciting and it has remained in the family memory as a great adventure. Of course you have to plan such a trip very carefully: if you have a car you have to have a way to get back to it two days later, and if you don't, you have to make sure of rail or bus connections to your next destination. Or you can make a round-trip backpacking expedition which will get you back to your starting point a few days later.

***   OTHER MOUNTAIN-RELATED SPORTS. There are some very exciting sports that go on in the mountains besides walking, climbing, rock-climbing and skiing. Even if you're not enthusiastic about these daring pursuits, you'll definitely enjoy watching them. At various times in the mountains I've seen people hang-gliding, parachuting, wafting in balloons and using gliders. Your teenager can take lessons in these, and go out with instructors. It's something very different—although you may draw the line at the more dangerous activities.

***   GUIDED MOUNTAIN EXPEDITIONS. After you and the family have done enough mountain walking to have confidence, you can try some more ambitious mountaineering. This is a mountain adventure that doesn't demand more technique than you have. There are mountains which are not intrinsically hard to climb—the distance from the start of the climb to the peak is something that you can handle and the grading is not too steep. But they're snow covered or you have to cross a glacier to get there. In this situation you know that you have the strength and stamina to do the walk, but you wouldn't want to cross the glacier unaided (you won't know where the crevasses might be) or you know that it would be more secure to be roped up on a snowy slope. Villages in the Rockies or the Alps and elsewhere have offices where you can hire guides for climbs. Discuss the difficulty of the walk for the members of your group with the guide. It's an exciting thing to do and will provide you and the family with some sense of the adventure that mountaineers feel when they're trying to climb more difficult peaks. The only thing that you would need would be a rope (usually provided by the guide) and possibly crampons (a form of cleats attached to your own boots that you can rent for a few dollars for the day). But you won't have to use any fancy climbing techniques. This will be an expensive treat—but your kids will love it!

Pregnant Women

Is it all right to do mountain walking when you are pregnant? The answer is that it can be problematic. The fetus could suffer from hypoxia (insufficient oxygen) at a high altitude. Doctors advise women to avoid visiting areas over 7,000–8,000 feet above sea level during pregnancy. (The situation is different if you actually live at this altitude. Your body should have learned to adjust.) While it should be all right to do mountain walking in the lower ranges during the first six months there is no good general rule. (I talk about this more in Chapter 9.) It's best to check with your doctor before making vacation plans.

Dogs

I don't know where in the family hierarchy dogs fit. They're less trouble than most children and more mature than many. They're certainly family members. Our experience has been that dogs love going to the mountains. And they're great fun to have along. Unless they're very small or very young, most dogs can keep up with anything you'll do in the mountains, short of rock climbing.

You'll also notice an interesting phenomenon. Many dogs have a shepherding instinct. If your family is strung out along a mountain path—maybe the older kids ahead and one of the parents behind with a little one—the dog will run back and forth, checking to see where everyone is and that they are going in the right direction. That's certainly what Babar, our medium-size poodle, did whenever we took him to the mountains. We reckoned that he did two or three times the amount of ascending and descending that the rest of us did. But he loved it.

Clearly, you have to have a responsible attitude when you walk with a dog in nature. Some national parks prohibit them altogether and you should check before making your plans. In other areas, local farmers want dogs on a leash during lambing time. You don't want your dog—even if you know he's totally harmless—to frighten other walkers on the path. You also don't want him to get into a tangle with a wild animal.

The Whole Family

A mountain vacation can be a wonderful experience to share with friends or family. Whether with a group of adults or a mix of grownups and children, doing things together can add a worthwhile dimension to a trip. The children can entertain one another, reducing the burden on the adults. And you can share out responsibilities—buying food, working out routes, looking after children.

Vacationing with a group is not always a picnic. You can get on each other's nerves or disagree on what you'd like to do. But that's the beauty of a walking holiday: you don't all have to stick together all the time. People can organize their own routes, team up with different members of the group each day, and adjust their itinerary to their needs and ability. Then, in the evening, you can all meet up and enjoy comparing notes, going out to dinner, having a beer in a local pub or doing whatever other activities are available where you're staying.

One thing is certain. While you'll be glad to go out at night for something to eat, chances are you won't want to stay up late. With the mountain air and the exercise that you're getting, you'll probably want to get to bed early. And you'll also be eager to wake up early the next morning and start another day of mountain adventure.

A Perfect Alpine Vacation

In this chapter I will take a single village in the Swiss Alps and go through a typical week of mountain hiking. Using the strengths you have on arrival, you will develop more skills gradually until you are ready for some ambitious climbs toward the end of your vacation there. The advice given here can be applied to a mountain vacation anywhere, Alps or Rockies, Dolomites or Green Mountains, Pyrenees or Adirondacks. So even if you have no intention of following me to this Swiss village, you can get a lot of general knowledge on how to organize a mountain adventure.

The Alps

What little girl has not grown up with the story and pictures of *Heidi*? The white-capped mountains, cozy wooden chalets, frisky goats, green, flowering meadows, bubbling streams: these are the images of the Alps that we carry with us. And they are not far from the truth.

Though for many the Alps are associated with Switzerland, in fact a number of countries share this impressive mountain range, the highest in Europe. France, Switzerland, Italy, Austria, Slovenia all have their own portion of the Alps. The magnificence of the Alps, their sheer grandeur and beauty in every season of the year draws people to them, whether they are climbers, walkers, skiers, or just tourists.

Flying over the Alps a passenger feasts her eyes on the overwhelming scene of high snow-covered mountains as far as the eye can see, glacial rivers, deep valleys speckled with villages. Even in summer, with all the pastures verdant and in bloom, the peaks are still white.

The Alps, like the Rockies, the Andes, and the Himalayas, were formed between thirty and sixty million years ago and have been subject to "only" a few million years of erosion. Being relatively young, they still maintain the more rugged, less eroded, form that differentiates them in shape from older mountains in Europe and North America. Walking up an Alpine slope may be steeper, but the hiker reaches her desired altitude more directly and covers less ground in doing so.

Climbing in the Alps—as in other high mountain ranges—provides a bird's-eye introduction to a variety of climatic zones and their vegetation. In a single day you can pass through the lowest level (the submontane zone) at your starting point—through the familiar plants of the coast and lower hills—up to the montane zone with its heavily forested areas. The top of the montane zone is marked by the end of the timber-line, or treeline. Beyond that, now in the alpine zone, trees cannot grow. This is the region of great pastureland filled with a remarkable display of all kinds of alpine flowers. Above this is the snow zone, a dramatic region where other plants and flowers are to be found, some even popping up through the melting snow. Every one of these zones has its own character and gradations and its own vegetation, something to be savored as you slowly make your way up from the lower to the higher altitudes.

The height of each zone differs from mountain range to mountain range, depending on the latitude. The lower the latitude, the higher you can go and still be below the timberline. So the high alpine zone in the Himalayas starts above 10,000 feet, whereas the treeline is already reached in varying places in the Rockies or the Alps at about 6,000 to 8,000 feet.

Visiting the Swiss Alps

It is because the Swiss have been hosts to mountain lovers for such a long time and have such a highly organized infrastructure for tourism that the beginning hiker can find it relatively easy to acclimate and to enjoy the physical and mental stimulation of the Alps. With the Swiss forests and mountains offering enchanting opportunities to appreciate nature, everything is done to enable the hiker to get onto the trail or up to higher places, or make good train or cable car connections with the least effort. This combination is what makes the many Swiss hill villages and towns so attractive for hikers, from the most to the least experienced.

The village we will be visiting is Zermatt, high up in the Alps almost equidistant from Zurich and Geneva, and about as far psychologically from the hubbub of city life as you can imagine. Like a few other Swiss villages—such as Wengen, Mürren, and Saas-Fee—Zermatt has outlawed any form of internal-combustion vehicles, so the only transportation within the village is by bicycle, little electric vans, and horse-drawn carriages. Nestled at the foot of the famous Matterhorn, this village is in the German-speaking province of Wallis (or Valais).

Getting There

Zermatt is reachable by train. At Brig you transfer to a funny little train at track 14, outside the station. (Coming from Geneva, you change at Visp.) It is very basic, no frills. While cars can drive part-way up, at some point the car has to be left in a lot and everyone piles into a train anyway.

On the window sill you'll find a panorama map indicating the 44 kilometer route that your train will now be taking, starting at Brig (elevation 672 meters) up to Zermatt at 1,602 meters.

It takes almost an hour and a half to make the twenty-seven and a half mile trip, as the train runs on cogs some of the way (to avoid slipping). When you reach Zermatt you will already be at over 5,000 feet altitude and your own climbing is yet to begin!

As height is given in meters in Europe, it is worthwhile to know that 1 meter = 3.28 feet. So if you want to know the height of Zermatt multiply 1,602 meters by 3.28, giving you Zermatt's altitude as 5,255 feet. To do it roughly in my head, I usually round out the number, multiply by 3 and add 10%.

Arriving

Coming into Zermatt after the long train trip is very exciting. All the way up during the last hour wonderful mountain views have unfolded as the train chugs upward. Once in the village you'll find yourself in the

A PERFECT ALPINE VACATION

bustle of a square where little electric vehicles can be
taken to your hotel or apartment. There are usually one
or two fine looking coaches
pulled by horses that service
two of the luxurious old
hotels that date from more
than a hundred years ago.

Whether you stay in a
chalet or a hotel, you are
likely to find the Swiss room
design refreshing: simple,
clean, with plenty of pine
wood, and firm beds covered
with big white comforters (or
what they call Fusskissen).
Drop your bags and take a
stroll through the village.

With just 5,500 inhabi-
tants, Zermatt is classified as
a village and it certainly has
the atmosphere of one, with
its narrow winding streets,
dark wooden houses, colorful
window boxes overflowing
with bright geraniums, and
little shops of every description. If you arrive in the
afternoon, you'll blend into
the flow of people who are
staying in the village: plenty

"We made Zermatt at three in the afternoon, nine hours out from St. Nicholas. Distance, by guide-book, twelve miles; by pedometer, seventy-two. We were in the heart and home of the mountain-climbers now, as all visible things testified. The snow-peaks did not hold themselves aloof, in aristocratic reserve; they nestled close around, in a friendly sociable way; guides, with the ropes and axes, and other implements of their fearful calling slung about their persons, roosted in a long line upon a stone wall in front of the hotel, and waited for customers; sun-burned climbers in moun-taineering costume, and followed by their guides and porters, arrived from time to time, from break-neck expeditions among the peaks and glaciers of the High Alps; male and female tourists, on mules, filed by in a continuous procession, hotelward-bound from wild adventures which would grow in grandeur every time they were described at the English or American fireside, and at last outgrow the possible itself."
—Mark Twain, A Tramp Abroad

of hikers still wearing their boots and carrying backpacks; summer
skiers wobbling on their clumsy plastic boots, skis on shoulders; weath-
ered climbers with heavy rope and ice axe hanging from their rucksacks; and the usual run of tourists (some even chicly dressed) there to
enjoy the breathtaking views and the mountain air. And the views are

Nepal: in the Lantang Valley

The Matterhorn

The Granite Mountains of Sinai

Trekking with camels in the Sinai Peninsula

Glacier National Park, Montana: an August snowfall

In the Grand Tetons, Wyoming

En route to Panch Pokari in the Himalayas

Dorje Lapka in the Jugal Himal, Nepal

Buttermere: the English Lake District

A rainbow over Ennerdale, the Lakes

On the way to Helvellyn, the Lakes

Late Spring in the Swiss Alps

Above Zermatt: the Monte Rosa massif

The summit of Mount Liberty in New Hampshire

The path disappears under leaves, New Hampshire

Fall in the White Mountains

truly amazing. Walk up the Bahnhofstrasse to the Parish church and turn left. Just as you cross the river, look to your right and see the reason that many thousands pour into Zermatt throughout the year: there, towering over the village, is the Matterhorn. Though there are many mountains in Switzerland—and even in the Zermatt region—that are over 12,000 feet high, no other carries the mystique of the Matterhorn or is as rec-ognizable, with its pointed top tilted off to one side. It is a magnet to moun-tain climbers and is also a great attraction to travelers in general. So there should be no surprise that almost every Japanese tour of Europe includes a stop in Zermatt, mainly for this spectacular view of the Matterhorn and the pleasure of being in a picture-perfect Swiss vil-lage surrounded by a ring of peaks over twelve-thousand feet high. There are thirty-six "four-thousanders"—mountains over 4,000 meters high—ringing Zermatt. The experience of being among so many snow-capped peaks is heady.

"[An] interesting woman arrived in Zermatt in 1871. Frances Ridley Havergal, the hymn writer, walked up from Visp to Randa and then obtained transport for the rest of the journey in a little horse-drawn carriage. . . . Miss Havergal was a frail, delicate creature, more than usu-ally subject to the vapours, rigours and declines which seem to have been continued

continued

lot of so many Victorian women. But the physical and spiritual climate of Zermatt had an amazing effect upon her and she performed feats which astonished herself as well as her friends. . . . In one of her letters she mentions her desire to climb the Cima di Jazzi and explains that the guide, in whom she had great confidence, was willing to accompany the party. Unfortunately, Miss Haveregal's friend had not been well and at the time of writing it was uncertain whether she would be able to make the trip. But Frances Ridley Havergal allayed any fears her family might have had that there would be an indiscreet trip. 'I am not so demented,' she wrote, 'as to go alone with a guide, without a lady companion.'"

—Cicely Williams

As you stroll through the village on your first afternoon you'll want to buy anything you may still need for tomorrow's walk: is there any equipment you need that you couldn't buy at home? Did you forget to bring a water bottle? Do you need gloves? Grease for your boots? Now is the time to pick up any missing items. This is also the time to buy a good map that shows trails and contours clearly. Besides this, get one of the cheap little 3D panoramic maps that will give you an idea, in picture form, of the routes you can take.

The Right Season in the Alps

The best time to walk in the Alps is the summer or the late spring and early fall. While trudging in the snow is great fun, it is a different sport. Early spring and late fall—while they can be very beautiful—often entail melting snow or muddy paths. Besides that, it is during these off-seasons that many hotels and restaurants close down.

Any time between late June and late September is exceptionally good for Alpine walking. If you are constrained by a school schedule you will probably be coming in July or August. (European families come in the second half of July and in August, when school is out.) If not, you may enjoy the somewhat quieter atmosphere of either the beginning or the end of season. Prices may be lower. While some restaurants may have closed (or not opened yet) and there is a little less bustle, you will still find plenty of charm in one of the Alpine villages to delight in.

"A walk from St. Nicholas to Zermatt is a wonderful experience. Nature is built on a stupendous plan in that region. One marches continually between walls that are piled into the skies, with their upper heights broken into a confusion of sublime shapes that gleam white and cold against the background of blue; and here and there one sees a big glacier displaying its grandeurs on the top of a precipice, or a graceful cascade leaping and flashing down the green declivities. There is nothing tame, or cheap, or trivial—it is all magnificent. That short valley is a picture gallery of a notable kind, for it contains no mediocrities; from end to end the Creator has hung it with His masterpieces."
—Mark Twain, 1880

There is no weather insurance, though. Unless you travel to an unusual place you can never be sure that there won't be rain. But you are taking this into account by bringing good rain garb with you. As a Swiss friend said recently: **"There is no such thing as bad weather; just bad clothes."**

The First Day's Walk

To start with, choose an easy or moderate walk. Every Alpine village offers a few choice starting walks. Even if you are in excellent condition, you will be using different muscles when you walk up and downhill and should get into climbing gradually. There are a few great walks in the Zermatt area that you can use to condition yourself. Every day you should plan to walk a little further and a little higher.

Get up early enough to make the most of the day. After breakfast put everything into your backpack, making sure that you don't forget any of the essentials. **Even if the weather looks good, put your rain gear in the bottom of your backpack, plus an extra sweater.** Remember that one characteristic of the mountains—anywhere—is that the weather can change. Fill your water bottle and put it in an outside pocket. Do you have bandages and corn pads handy? Your folding knife for lunch should be in easy reach. Is your map accessible? Take money and your camera. And always take your rail pass with you, just in case you need it.

A PERFECT ALPINE VACATION

Put the backpack on and make sure that it is well adjusted. The finest of packs will be uncomfortable if not fitted correctly. Today's backpacks have countless ways to make adjustments—almost too many, because everything adds to the weight. Make sure that the shoulder straps are the right length. They shouldn't cut into you. **The weight of the pack should be well distributed** so that it falls not only on your shoulders but also on your back and even on your hips. If your pack has a belt at the waist, try fastening it to see if it is comfortable and helps spread the weight. (While this may seem exaggerated, given the relatively small amount you have inside, I can assure you that as you climb, the pack does seem to grow heavier!) Look in the mirror and see if the pack looks balanced; you don't want it listing to one side.

You should now be ready to go out, wearing a t-shirt (and possibly something over it, depending on the weather) plus your wind jacket. If your boots are pretty new, give them a good look now because they won't ever look like this again. Stop by whatever local shops are nearby—there are plenty of bakeries in the village and a number of food stores—and (for two) get fresh rolls, 200–300 grams of one of the good local cheeses, a couple of apples and—if you like—a chocolate bar and whatever snack food (nuts, raisins) you've decided on. Most of the stores also sell hard-boiled eggs, if you prefer one for lunch. Many of the Swiss guides prefer to take along a good sausage, or wurst, for their meal. All of this should be packed in toward the top of your bag.

Up to Z'mutt. **This is a perfect first-day walk and is the kind that you should take wherever you are starting your hiking. It includes an ascent of a thousand feet, varied scenery, splendid views and a good place to stop at the top.** You can pick up the path just beyond the Church square. There are a number of ways to take initially. Don't be put off by the wooden directional signs. The one just past the church says that the way to Z'mutt (pronounced "tsmoot") is "1 std", one hour, and after six or eight minutes of walking you'll come across another sign with the same timing. The problem of timing on signs exists all over and you should avoid putting too much stock by them.

The route provides a long steady ascent, initially past some gravel piles. Below you on the left you'll see the river and the cable cars swinging out toward Zum See and Furi. This is a route where you're likely to find lots of people: it's the classic Zermatt walk, not too demanding but scenic. You will even find occasional benches along the way. Don't use them!

Get yourself into a comfortable gait and walk steadily at a speed that does not strain you and feels right. You shouldn't make stops, but should try to keep your pace even. Don't slow down and then put on speed to catch up. Steady does it.

PACE

There is a gradual climb, which you will start to feel if you are not in top condition. Find a speed that does not make you breathless. **If you are walking with others, let them do the talking until you are sure that you're not out of breath.** People easily get winded, usually because they have pushed themselves too hard. The beauty of mountain walking is that you can choose your own speed.

There are two ways to handle the need to walk slowly and steadily if

"Slow and steady wins the race," *said the Tortoise to the Hare.*

you are not alone. One is to go at your own speed and to meet up later. The other, if you prefer to stay together, is to let the weaker hiker set the pace. Let her be the first one in line and whoever else there is can fall in after her. If you put your weakest walker at the end of the line, she may try to push herself too hard in order to keep up, or she may be discouraged and fall back. **Don't be forced into going at a faster pace than is comfortable.**

Altitude can have a role in your feeling of strain when walking uphill. At a little over five thousand feet, Zermatt falls into the category of a city like Denver, where people sometimes feel the height after arrival. However, flying into Denver is different from taking hours in a train chugging up to Zermatt. The more gradual attainment of height probably makes it easier to acclimate to Zermatt.

For part of the way up, clouds permitting, you get fine views of the Matterhorn. With all the twists and turns, you'll often lose sight of it, but then there will be a full view again when you reach Z'mutt.

After the last swing of the path, you will suddenly see a couple of clusters of buildings a ten-minute walk ahead, with Swiss flags flying. A tiny white plaster church stands in among a restaurant or two. Almost every Swiss hike ends with the Swiss flag and this will come to represent a welcome symbol to you. You'll know that your climb is at an end, that a bowl of hot vegetable soup and a place to sit are waiting.

Even at an elevation of one thousand feet, put on a jacket or an extra sweater when you sit down. Take it off again when you start walking. Whenever you reach a high point and stop walking, put on extra clothing, even if you feel warm from the effort of getting there.

ETIQUETTE

Find a place at one of the tables and enjoy a cold bottled drink or some hot soup or coffee. In restaurants like these, as they are so close to Zermatt, it's not necessarily acceptable to pull your food out of your

"We were approaching Zermatt, consequently we were approaching the renowned Matterhorn. . . . We were expecting to recognize that mountain whenever or wherever we should run across it. We were not deceived. The monarch was far away when we first saw him, but there was no such thing as mistaking him. He has the rare peculiarity of standing by himself. He is peculiarly steep, too, and is also most oddly shaped. He towers into the sky like a colossal wedge, with the upper third of its blade bent a little to the left. The broad base of this monster wedge is planted upon a grand glacier-paved Alpine platform whose elevation is ten thousand feet above sea level. So the whole bulk of this stately piece of rock, this sky-cleaving monolith, is above the line of eternal snow. Yet while all its giant neighbours have continued

backpack and spread it out on the table. The best thing to do is to ask. If you are ordering something, the restaurant may not mind if you also eat your own food there, but they may. Excellent food can be served at these mountain restaurants: besides homemade soups, there are fine omlettes and hash-browned potatos (a fantastic Swiss version of them called Rösti), quiches, and hearty sandwiches. You may decide that some days you'll carry your lunch and on other days opt for restaurant fare.

continued

the look of being built of solid snow, from their waists up, the Matterhorn stands black and naked and forbidding the year round, or merely powdered or streaked with white in places, for its sides are so steep that the snow cannot stay there. Its strange form, its august isolation, and its majestic unkinship with its own kind, make it, so to speak, the Napoleon of the mountain world. 'Grand, gloomy, and peculiar,' is a phrase which fits it as aptly as it fitted the great captain."
—Mark Twain, 1880

RETURN TO ZERMATT

You can return to Zermatt the way you came. Everything looks different in reverse so the walk will still be interesting. Or you can choose a different route. This will give you a chance to see something new and that's always an attractive alternative. However you

RULES FOR THE INEXPERIENCED CLIMBER:
- *Walk slowly and steadily*
- *Don't keep stopping*
- *Do not take frequent breaks for food or drink*
- *Drink enough to avoid dehydration*
- *Save your breath while walking uphill: don't talk too much!*
- *Let the weakest walker set the pace for herself or for the group*
- *Shed clothes as you climb*
- *Put on warm clothes when you stop*

go, your total amount of walking on the first day will have been between two and three hours, including a thousand feet up and down. Not bad.

When you are finished with a walk, the best thing to do is to go back to your hotel or apartment. You'll want to change your clothes and before you do that **you should have a hot bath**. The bath is not just for getting clean: even if you are a convinced showerer, when you are hiking—if you have the good fortune to have a tub—you should soak in hot water after you come down off the trail. It helps your muscles to relax and wards off a certain amount of aching either immediately or by the next morning. This is not just a luxury. In fact, you may even want to take another hot bath later at night, before you go to bed.

This reminds me that on one of our first vacations in Switzerland—and this was in Grindelwald—my husband and I missed the train coming down off the Jungfraujoch and we ended up dashing down the mountainside in order to get back into the village to pick up some pictures before the photography store closed. We really ran. When we got to the store, I sat down while waiting for the clerk to find the films and by the time he had found them, I could hardly get up. I was that stiff! Going home first and having a hot bath would have done us out of the films till the next day, but it certainly would have eased my over-stressed muscles.

GOOD FIRST DAY WALKS:
Z'mutt
Edelweiss
Findeln
Ritti

The Second Day's Walk

Even if you wake up in the morning with some muscle ache, don't let that bother you: you can walk it out and within a day or two you should have no discomfort at all.

Before you put on your boots in the morning, think about your feet. Did you have any problems with them on the first day? Did you have to stop to put on any bandages? Remember that *if you have any pressure on any part of your foot, or blisters or corns, stop your walk immediately, sit down in a comfortable place, and bandage whatever part of your foot that hurts.* Never wait until the end of the walk. Never postpone taking care of your feet, even if the pain comes at an inconvenient time or place. You will avoid far worse trouble later by doing this. Likewise, in the morning if you have a sore spot, use some of your bandages or pads before you put on your socks and boots. If you have to add more bandages in the course of the day, they're in your backpack.

After breakfast, you'll have the same routine as on the first day: put everything into your backpack and pick up a few items for your lunch on your way out of the village.

Uphill to the Edelweiss and Beyond

If you didn't start out your vacation in good shape and feel that the walk to Z'mutt was as strenuous as you wanted, then spend another day on a short walk, with another 1,000-foot climb and just go as far as the Edelweiss. But if you did well yesterday, today your walk should be longer and higher. This route takes you in a different direction and with another set of views. It makes an excellent second day hike.

Look for signs in the village toward Edelweiss and Trift. It should take about an hour to do the 1,000-foot climb to Edelweiss (though at least one of the signs says three-quarters of an hour—maybe you'll do it in that time later in the week when you've picked up speed!). This walk is pretty much a direct ascent to a little spot almost exactly above Zermatt. In the beginning you will zigzag up past houses to a steep meadow. If you come early in the summer—that is, late June or early July—the meadows will be full of flowers of every kind. Later, the meadow— grass and flowers—will be cut for hay. This isn't to say that you don't see flowers over the course of the summer, but the big show is before the first cutting.

Among the flowers there that are easily recognizable in the Edelweiss area:
Forget-me-nots
Daisies
Buttercups
Gentian
Orchids
Pinks
Clover
Alpine roses
Dandelions
Violets

As the path winds its way through the meadow the whole of Zermatt gradually becomes visible: roofs, church, tennis courts. Later you reach the pine forest, mainly larch, on the steep rocky side of the mountain. Although the path is well-marked, it's always prudent to take your route map with you. You'll cross two wooden bridges and then reach the rushing stream, which will reappear at various times during the day. At the top of the steep path you reach the Edelweiss, which suddenly appears just above you. The pale pink little hotel/restaurant is a landmark in the Zermatt area, visible from the village and a first stop on many longer routes. At night you can see its light shining through the darkness. If you want a little break—or a lavatory—stop at the Edelweiss and enjoy the truly spectacular view down to the village and out toward a number of mountains, including the Breithorn straight ahead and, around to the left, the Taeschhorn and the Dom—and far below, the Rhone Valley. People love to sit outside on the little stone terrace soaking in sun and views.

On to Trift
The next leg of the walk (unless you decide that enough is enough) takes you cross-country away from the Zermatt side. From the Edelweiss on, you are now above the treeline. Follow the sign to Trift just past the restaurant. It's a varied walk and full of sights, with another thousand feet to climb over the next hour. The path gradually ascends over narrow pasture land, zigzagging up. Below you to the right is the rushing torrent, which you eventually cross when you are about halfway up. After the bridge a new vista gradually opens. Now you can see the Trifthorn, the Obergabelhorn, the Wellenkuppe, and the Zinal Rothorn, each with their distinct shapes, which you will start to recognize. With Zermatt behind and out of sight well below you, the wall of mountains ahead provides a dramatic view of glaciers, the ice rivers that move down mountains at slower than a snail's pace. This is a totally different sight from the lush valley you have just left: a domain of ice and snow and jagged peaks. In an hour and a half of walking you have entered an entirely new realm, attainable only by foot and offering a wealth of frigid beauty for the hiker. Though there may be another walker or two on the path ahead or behind, you will pretty much have it to yourself.

The walk up to Trift will be demanding, but worth it. The path is excellent. You should now have established a good pace for yourself and be walking with a steady rhythm. Remember not to rush: you'll get to Trift in roughly the time indicated on the signs and will find another little restaurant waiting. Quite a long time before you get there, you'll see the Swiss flag flying at Trift.

The restaurant itself is on a little plateau with the path you have just climbed barely visible down to the left. But facing you is a high grass-covered slope, crisscrossed with paths and contrasting with the icy hauteur of the glacial scene to the right. By the time you get to Trift, you have shed the strollers seeking a view just above the village and are in real walking—and climbing—country. From here, some climbers will be heading towards the Rothorn hut to ascend the Wellenkuppe, the Zinal Rothorn, or the Obergabelhorn. Others will be heading towards the Mettelhorn to complete a fine climb of six thousand feet, with no ropes necessary. Make a mental note of that for a superb walk toward the end of your stay.

To return to Zermatt you can either take the same path down to Edelweiss and beyond again or, if you've got an excess of energy, take the longer way down. For this, you should climb up the meadowland above Trift following a sign that points out a path to "Zermatt: two hours." This route takes you up another few hundred feet and then follows a very steep way down, past large permanent structures designed to prevent avalanches during the snowy season, and eventually zigzagging across the side of the mountain, looking down on Zermatt as you approach it. If you don't like steep inclines, or aren't quite ready for one, this round-trip alternative isn't for you. Downhill walking can be felt in the toes, knees, calves, and thighs. But the more you use your muscles, the less you will eventually feel them.

Walking on the Third Day

We'll head in yet a different direction for new perspectives and another glorious walk, longer and higher. By the third day, you should feel comfortable heading out in the morning, backpack full of whatever you'll need. This walk will not only provide a day's worth of beautiful sights, but will also dip into a bit of Zermatt history.

The first part of the walk takes you up two thousand feet to Riffelalp. Don't be fooled by the sign you may see promising a one hour walk: it will take you roughly two hours to climb it at normal speed. The route starts up to Winkelmatten, a suburb perched just above Zermatt (if villages can be said to have suburbs), so it's a steep start. After that, you climb up through dense forest, which is so beautifully landscaped by nature that at times you feel that you are in a magnificent rock garden. On this route, as on others, you will come across a variety of birds and perhaps have the pleasure of hearing the unmistakable sound of the cuckoo.

At 2,222 meters (7,288 feet), Riffelalp rests on a flat landing part way up to higher climbs. When I first walked up to Riffelalp with my family twenty-five years ago, we found a small restaurant there that served walkers and also some old empty buildings that always roused our curiosity. One of the buildings looked as if it had been a large hotel. The other was a little Anglican church. Both were shut up tight. They were reminders of a by-gone era.

Over 150 years ago, small numbers of intrepid English tourists (the main group among various European visitors) began to make their way to Zermatt. Both men and women would come up to the tiny village to spend the summer tramping over the unspoiled and exceedingly beautiful mountains above the settlement. In the beginning there were only a handful of tourists and almost no accommodation in the village. Gradually hotels were built to serve the growing number of visitors. An Anglican church was put up behind the main street (the Bahnhofstrasse) for the English vacationers who sought fresh air, natural beauty and a physical challenge. One of the earlier hotels (at first no more than a climbing hut) was built a couple of thousand feet above the village, at Riffelalp and, together with it, a small church for the many English tourists who were coming to the sunny Alpine slopes. Later, a cogwheel railway heading up to the

> *"Miss Havergal . . . described the English church which had been built about 1870 and had been discussed by the Alpine Club for some years before that. In those days the Englishman liked to find his church awaiting him when he arrived for his holiday."*
> —Cicely Williams, 1871

Gornergrat high above would stop not far from Riffelalp and a little electric tram (inaugurated in 1899) would then take the visitors and their trunks and cases the short distance to the hotel itself. From Riffelalp a large number of higher altitude walks as well as climbs could be commenced.

Today, British tourists are only the fifth largest group coming to Zermatt in the summer: before them are, in order, the Swiss, Germans, Japanese, and Americans. The Anglican church in the village is still in use. My husband and I attended a moving service of the Alpine Club there in the 1980s. One of the speakers was Lord John Hunt, who had organized the first successful expedition to climb Mount Everest. He arrived in Zermatt for the meeting having crossed by foot from Saas-Fee, over the high glacier—at the age of 78!

The hotel at Riffelalp, which so warmly received its guests a hundred years ago has now been completely and luxuriously refurbished and hosts both walkers in the summer and skiers in the winter. It makes a very suitable stopping place on your way, though perhaps too early for lunch. If you are vacationing with children or others who might not want to overdo their walking, you have some good choices: they can either walk up with you to Riffelalp and then take the train back down to Zermatt, or they can take the train up to Riffelalp and then continue with you on your walk. **When visiting the mountains with others, try to arrange alternative ways to reach the same place and to satisfy the needs of those who want to do a good day's walking and those who may not be able to expend as much energy.**

From Riffelalp, proceed to Grünsee, under an hour away, with a gentle incline and a very fine change of views. Only 374 feet higher, this will be an easy part of the day. The hotel and restaurant at Grünsee, like so many such places in the Zermatt area, has a large sun terrace where you can enjoy lunch or a drink. Ten minutes beyond the restaurant is the actual Grünsee: a small green-tinged lake that attracts many walkers and picknickers. From there you can see a new array of mountains: the Rimpfischhorn, the Strahlhorn, and Alphubel and then down to the fresh green meadows of Sunnegga and Findeln.

Again, if part of your group are weaker walkers, they can re-trace their footsteps to Riffelalp and take the train down to the village. But by this time, you should find your hiking much easier and can return by a longer route, enjoying new views. This will take you down into the woods again and then, crossing a stream, up a little bit to the tiny village of Findeln, houses dotting the hillside and with a few choice places to stop again if you are in the mood. From Findeln down to Zermatt it should take you about an hour. So all in all your walking today will include a climb of a little over two thousand feet and about five hours of walking. You'll get back down in plenty of time for a hot bath and a stroll through the village before a good dinner.

If you've got excess energy there are a number of good tennis courts in the center of town or you can have a swim in one of the hotels.

A Good Fourth Day's Walk

These walks have been organized to give you a gradual increase in walking time and height reached as well as to send you in diverse

TAKING A BREAK FROM WALKING

Active Options:
   Tennis
   Swimming
   Mule trekking
   Mountain biking
   Rock climbing clinic
   Other technique classes
   Skiing (at high altitude)
   Visit the glacier schlucht

Less Active Options:
   Glacier Express: take a train ride!
   Visit the English Church
   Visit the Alpine Museum
   Take a lift or cable car
   Wellness centers (Jacuzzi, sauna)
   Knitting Shop (if you're into knitting)
   Visit the mountaineers' cemetery
   Cafes, pubs, shopping

directions—you will never have the feeling that you are doing the same walk over and over. This is a good principle whenever you plan for a period of time in the mountains: **look at the map and work out routes that will provide you with incremental strength and variety.** It's very easy in a place like Zermatt. We have spent weeks at a time there and taken a different walk every day.

Today the route goes up to the Schwartzsee with a climb of about 3,200 feet. The start of the walk follows the signs toward Furi, but then branches off and heads into the forest. You'll get to about the same height as Z'mutt and be able to look across toward it before you cross the road and head up toward Hermettje which, at 2,027 meters (almost 1,400 feet above Zermatt), is a good place for a stop and a view. This is just one of the possible routes up to the Schwartzsee, but a very good one. Above Hermettje, the path zigzags up through the trees. Depending upon when you are there, you may see Alpine roses or other wild flowers. About three-quarters of an hour before the top you will find yourself above the treeline, on pasture land with an abundance of little flowers. It is in this area that I have seen marmots, the little furry animals that are typical of the Zermatt area.

Near the Schwartzsee (which is a disappointingly small lake) a glorious spectacle opens up: across the valley is the frozen panorama of the Monte Rosa, the highest mountain of the region, the great mass of mountain and the pure white of the glacier.

If you like picturesque names, these flowers are all in the Zermatt area:

Bearded Bellflower
Golden Hawksbeard
Swiss Treacle-mustard
Alpine Birdsfoot Trefoil
Lousewort
Globe-headed Rampion
Alpine Snowbell
Longspurred Pansy
Cobweb Houseleek
Hairy Spurred Milkwort

From here, too, you can see the path winding up to the Hornlihutte, where climbers commence their assault on the Matterhorn. If you have an abundance of energy, you can climb another couple of thousand feet up the steep path for two hours to visit the hut, which has a restaurant. Then come down again to the Schwartzsee and take the cable car from there to Zermatt. Otherwise, the Schwartzsee itself is an excellent target for the day. There are different ways down but if it's late or you feel that that's enough—the cable car is right there.

Reminders
1. Every day you should bring all your gear, bandages, snacks.
2. Use sunscreen on sunny days, even if the air temperature seems comfortably cool.
3. Change into other shoes and socks after you return to your hotel each day and let your boots dry and air out.

If It Rains
A few drops shouldn't bother you. But if you have the impression that it's really beginning to rain, stop walking, pull out your raingear and put it on. Once you get thoroughly wet, putting on rainproof pants over your slacks will only make you uncomfortable. **So put on your rainproof clothing in time.** That's why you've been carrying it!

After four days' good walking, once you have made it to the Schwartzsee you are capable of pretty much any walking on the Zermatt area paths. You can now look for more challenges, either in distance or height: the sky's the limit!

Going Further Afield

Although there are still plenty of walks to do right from Zermatt, there are also splendid routes easily accessible if you take the train. Zermatt is at the head of a long valley and all along the way down toward Brig there are villages that have their own complex of paths up other mountains. Once you have a Swiss Card, you can take the train at half price a stop or two down the mountain, pick up a path out of Taesch, Randa, St. Niklaus, or Kalpetran and then return by train at the end of the day.

Alternatively, you can walk out of Zermatt on a fine path and end up, by foot, lower down the valley and take the train back. One wonderful walk of that kind is up to Taeschalp over the Sattel, reached by walking through Tuftern (again, a new direction for you) and then further north. Reaching the Sattel, above the treeline, perched on a rocky pass, you can catch terrific mountain views in a number of directions, and then proceed down through a cow meadow to Taeschalp, still very high up, with just a café and a few vacation houses. Climbers continue from there to the Taesch hut, another good hike. But for the Sattel walk, the path continues from Taeschalp down through a rich forest (where occasional deer can be spotted) to the village of Taesch, where you can catch a train for the ten-minute ride back up to Zermatt. Or you can reverse the order and take the train to Taesch in the morning and walk up to the Taesch hut to get a view of one of the huts—like the Hörnli hut—where climbers start their ascent of higher mountains. I personally love the walk from Tuftern to the Sattel because of its views and the

> *"Even ladies catch the climbing mania, and are unable to throw it off. A famous climber of that sex had attempted the Weisshorn a few days before our arrival, and she and her guides had lost their way in a snowstorm high up among the peaks and glaciers, and been forced to wander around a good while before they could find a way down. When this lady reached the bottom she had been on her feet twenty-three hours!"*
>
> —Mark Twain, 1880

variety of the walk. It is one of the few places that I've ever come across the Edelweiss—the famous snowy little wild flower of Switzerland, a protected species—growing in nature.

Here are another couple of suggested walks outside Zermatt that include the use of transportation. There are many more.

Jungu

Start out by taking the train from Zermatt down to St. Niklaus, which has an altitude of 1,100 meters. The walk more or less straight out of the St. Niklaus station takes you up to the tiny village of Jungu at 1,958 meters, a climb of about 2,800 feet. The route has a special component. The canton of Valais is Catholic and it is not unusual to find crucifixes or little chapels when you are walking in the mountains here. But this particular path is more like a pilgrimage route with a series of little white shrines, too small to enter, all along the way. Each one has a wooden carving with a scene from the New Testament that can be seen through the grating. These roadside sculptures start with a scene preceding the birth of Jesus and go on through

An excerpt from Psalm 36 at one of the stations on the way up to Jungu: *"Thy righteousness is like the great mountains; thy judgments are a great deep: O Lord, thou preservest man and beast."*

events in his life, ending with one of him in heaven.

The route itself is very beautiful, clearly marked and with an occasional steeper gradient. You find yourself going up and up above St. Niklaus and getting varied views of life in the long valley below. Spread out below you, like a child's toy model of Switzerland, are little villages, picture-book chalets, a coursing river the width of a finger tumbling down toward the Rhone, a thread-like road with a few miniature cars, and the railroad. The sound of the bells from St. Niklaus reaches far up into the hills.

Jungu is no more than a dot on a highly detailed map, but a lovely and pastoral spot to arrive at. You may well see a farmer with a scythe out in his field, or cows grazing. A restaurant situated among some farm houses is a welcoming sight as well. There is a charming little church in Jungu with a remarkable brightly-painted wooden altarpiece. Throughout the Alps generally, you can be on the lookout for special places to stop at, not just the peaks.

From Jungu you can either walk down or, if you are pressed for time, there is an unusual cable car that takes

SOUNDS ON AN ALPINE WALK
Bubbling streams
Sheep baa-ing
Birds
Church bells
Waterfalls
Cow bells
Crunch of boots on the path
Squoosh of boots on spongy ground

you straight down to St. Niklaus. Only four people can sit in it at a time and it runs on a self-service basis. A schedule informs when the cable car can be expected and the ride down is great fun. But if there are a few people ahead of you, you'll have to wait for the next one. You pay at the bottom.

If you want to extend your walk by another two and a half hours, then continue from Jungu along to Embd. From there you can take a different cable car down to Kalpetran and then the train back to Zermatt. These suggestions should give you an idea of the number of variations that are possible when planning your route.

ANOTHER POINT OF ETIQUETTE

If you find yourself on a narrow path, or are facing a tricky clamber over rocks, and someone comes up from behind and is just about to overtake you, step aside and let them pass. If you're on that same narrow path and people are approaching from the opposite direction, in general the people who are ascending are given the right of way if there's really only room for one at a time. It may be that you're the one coming uphill and you'd welcome a moment's rest. In that case, step aside anyway. The main thing is to use your common sense.

Saas Fee

This is a truly spectacular walk and takes you from the Zermatt valley over to another beautiful village some eight hours walk away. So leave Zermatt as early as possible. Keep in mind what time it gets dark and plan your day accordingly. **You do not want to get caught on any mountain after nightfall.**

> **BIRDS AND ANIMALS IN THE ALPS**
> *Not only are there flowers, but you'll also find the woods full of birdsong. If you're lucky, here are some of the birds and animals you may spot:*
> Birds: *Woodpeckers, sparrows, owls of various kinds, eagles, ravens, nutcrackers, wall creepers, grouse.*
> Animals: *Marmots, hares, red foxes, badgers, various deer, ibex, chamois.*

In terms of transportation, the route includes everything: a train from Zermatt to St. Niklaus, a bus from St. Niklaus to Grachen, a cable car (a gondola for six) up 1,500 feet to Hannigalp at 2,121 meters. The highest point on the walk is 2,670 meters, or a climb of only 1,800 feet from Hannigalp, though you will be going up and down a bit, so that the total amount "climbed" will be more. Because the walk is very long, you should only do it if you feel you have adequate stamina. It is certainly well worth the effort.

The route, very well marked, also includes every kind of experience: passing under the Balfrin Glacier at the beginning of the day, then the Bider Glacier and later the Hohbalm Glacier near Saas Fee; two traverses across massive rock slides, stepping from one boulder to the next; crossing more than one turbulent stream that is rushing down to join the Sasser Vispa River; using fixed rope railings in a number of tricky spots; and seeing magnificent views. The Bernese Oberland now comes into view with a whole new set of mountains. The last time I did this walk we spotted deer on two occasions.

If you are new to mountain walking, there are a few points to note.

WATCHING THE PATH

1. The path is very narrow in places (some five boot-widths across) so that in many places you are walking with the mountainside to your right and a precipitous drop to the left. If you are sure-footed and have a good head for heights this will not hamper you at all. But, if you suffer from vertigo when you find yourself on a narrow ledge, this path may not be for you. In general, in walking on narrow paths with deep drops on one or both sides, you should keep your eyes focused ahead of you and watch where you are going. Looking down into the abyss—unless you actually stop to enjoy the view—is not good policy.
2. There are roots on the path in some places—as in many walks. If they are wet, you should avoid stepping on them when you can, as they can be very slippery.
3. In the places where you have to cross over sloping rocks, you will be able to cope with this as long as your boots have good treads. In hiking, you have to learn to count on your boots.
4. In walking down steep dry rocks, put your entire foot firmly on the stone. Don't walk heel-toe as you usually do. The more shoe surface you have on the rock, the more secure you are.

Remember that it will take you the better part of a day to reach Saas Fee and that there are no restaurants or toilets along the way. So don't forget to use the facilities at the gondola station. You will definitely have to take lunch with you and, if it's hot, extra water.

Besides the natural beauty of the route, you will find walking through the woods above Saas Fee during the last hour a feast for the eyes: thick forest abounding in magnificent Alpine roses.

One caveat is in order. If you are thinking of doing this walk before mid-July it is important to check which days the gondola is in use from Grachen up to Hannigalp. Early in the season it does not run every day and if you don't take it, you will be adding yet another hour and a half to your day's walking.

Saas Fee itself is a delightful find at the end of the day: a charming village filled with shops and cafes, bustling with hikers, and, like Zermatt, free of any vehicles except horse-drawn or electric ones. Find out when the bus at the edge of the village can get you to Stalden, where you will catch your train to Zermatt. Or stay overnight and return the next day.

Two Classic Longer Walks in the Zermatt Area

Toward the end of the week think about taking on a really challenging walk. There are two superb long climbs that will crown your visit.

Gornergrat

The very top of the cogwheel rail system starting out from Zermatt and passing Riffelalp, Riffelberg, and Rotenboden, is the Gornergrat. It can be seen from some distance, with its recognizable observatory dome and large hotel building on a snowy ledge. There are various ways to do the five thousand-foot/five-hour climb. Check your map and choose a good route. My favorite is to re-trace your walk from the third day and continue from the Grünsee straight up, following the signpost opposite the restaurant. The day's walk will give you everything a good mountain itinerary can offer: a forest walk early in the day, open meadow high above Grünsee, myriad field flowers, a bubbling stream to picnic by, towering mountains in all directions, ponds, and, possibly—even in the summer—a snow field to cross. The view at the top is breathtaking. You have transported yourself in five hours of walking to a world of snow and ice. There before you is the huge mass of the Monte Rosa, glaciers spilling down, the pyramid-shaped Matterhorn, standing on its own, and a host of other mountains. Cover up and walk around the whole area of the Gornergrat soaking in the beauty of it all. This is truly a visual feast.

After walking around at the top and having a hot drink inside, you will probably want to take the train down, as the return walk takes another few hours.

Mettelhorn

By the end of a week's walking, you may be ready for another fine walk that will present a challenge: climbing the Mettelhorn. This is an 11,000 foot mountain that can be climbed entirely by foot, without a guide and without rock climbing paraphernalia. The climb itself is 6,000 feet. As the route is away from the train line, you have to both ascend and descend by foot. It is a good idea to check in at the guides' office in the center of the village to ask about conditions on the Mettelhorn before you go. The route is fine for strong walkers, but not advisable if you have not built up sufficient stamina or feel uncomfortable on snow.

Take the second day's path up to Trift and from there follow the signposts to the Mettelhorn. This beautiful walk has an unusual end: after crossing a large area of meadow above the tree line, you will eventually come to a snow field and a glacier. These have to be crossed and you may feel more comfortable taking a walking stick with you or an ice axe to chop steps in the snow as required. An ice axe or walking stick can be rented in the village for a small fee. After crossing the snow, you then come to what looks like a pile of rocks, and to reach the top of the mountain you must climb this too. The last lap takes another twenty or thirty minutes. When you reach the summit, you will find yourself on top of the world, perched on a rock, looking out at the vast scene around and beneath you. Sitting up there, bundled up and enjoying the view and a snack, you will see birds swooping around below, a rare pleasure.

Going back will take you a somewhat shorter time. In general, unless there is a very tricky descent going down takes perhaps twenty-five percent less time than climbing up.

Women Walking in the Zermatt Area

From some of the quotations sprinkled throughout this chapter you can see that since its beginning as a mountaineering center a hundred fifty years ago, Zermatt has attracted women walkers. This is true today, even if the men may still outnumber us. There is a general feeling that there is no problem in being a woman walking alone—little or no more than a man alone. There is a very low crime rate there. **It is inadvisable, however, for anyone to go on a very long or arduous walk alone unless you are very experienced.** Even if you are, it is customary to tell someone—for example the desk at your hotel—where you are going and when you expect to be back. This is a safety measure for anyone going out on a difficult walk.

Walking with a Baby

If you are in Zermatt with a baby and want to get in some good walking, you have two possibilities, if you choose to take the baby with you. One is to carry the baby in a sling or pouch or papoose. This is discussed in Chapter 7. There are reasons that you may not choose this option:

1. The baby is not happy in a pouch or papoose. (Rachel's baby, for instance, refused to rest calmly in a frontal pouch though many babies love them.)
2. You are not comfortable carrying that way.
3. The baby will be calmer—or sleep better—if he is lying down in a carriage.

If you prefer to have your baby lie down, there are at least two good walks that you can do out of Zermatt, pushing a carriage. In either case—carrying or pushing—remember that there's a lot more work involved than in walking on your own. Ideally, you should be able to switch off and share the burden with at least one other person. (If your baby is already sitting, a three-wheeled stroller that's much easier to use in the mountains can be rented in the village.)

1. One possibility is to go to Tuftern, which has all the pleasures of a good mountain walk, culminating in a spectacular view of the Matterhorn at the top. The regular footpath goes up through the woods and is highly recommended for a two-hour walk up. But if you want to push a carriage it takes more stamina and a slightly different route. Take the unpaved road through Ried,

just following the signs to Tuftern. It is now used for mountain biking as well. It's a bit more roundabout but suitable for a carriage or stroller and offers much of the beauty of the forest walk. The climb is about two thousand feet, a pretty good workout for a woman with a carriage. (Both my daughters have managed this with their firstborns, taking turns at pushing every ten minutes with someone else.) At Tuftern you can eat and will find someplace for changing diapers and so on. It's a lovely spot and you will enjoy the unparalleled view. From there you can either retrace your steps or walk another half hour or so to Sunnegga and take the little tunnel train back down to Zermatt.

2. A second good walk with a carriage or stroller is up to Furi, again along a quiet road. Here there is less of a climb—about a thousand feet up—but still picturesque—surrounding mountains, villages dotting the valley, restaurants to stop at. It certainly gives you a good alternative and the opportunity to return by cable car if you choose. If you have more energy, you can continue up the road past Furi to a spot higher up at Staffelalp. This would give you a total of 2,000 feet up for the day, the same as walking to Tuftern, though a gentler rise over a longer route.

Again, if you are traveling with children there are babysitters available through a listing at the Tourist Information Office near the train station in Zermatt. Even if you want to take the kids with you during the day, you may want a quiet couple of hours at dinnertime.

During the daytime there are organized children's activities from 2 to 4 P.M. for children in the three to seven year range. For older children there are other activities.

Earlier in this chapter (page 114), I listed a variety of activities available in the area for active and non-active people. For active sports such as summer skiing or a rock climbing class, get in touch with the guides office in the middle of the village. You may well have fallen under the spell of the Alps after spending a few days there walking and want to explore the other aspects of Alpine adventure. A half-day class with a good teacher can instill good mountain-climbing techniques and initiate you in the ways of abseiling and rapelling: using ropes to climb and descend rock face.

By the end of your stay you may also feel ready—and eager—to take a guide or join a group to climb one of the more accessible mountains that are a step more than simple hiking uphill. Get the experience of being roped up, of using crampons if you are attracted to it. A whole new world of snow, rock, and ice will open up for you!

Summing Up

Use this description of Zermatt and the walking schedule as a proto-type, even if you don't literally follow it on a trip to Switzerland. You can adhere to the general concepts anywhere:

1. Plan your route carefully in advance.
2. Check on the weather forecast before you set out, particularly with regard to possible storms.
3. Bring sufficient food and water for the day.
4. Carry all the foot care and other provisions mentioned in Chapter 6.
5. Start out early, to make the most of the day.
6. Establish a steady pace for yourself and stick to it. Don't keep stopping to rest.
7. Take care to plan a walk that will get you back well before dark.
8. Work out a schedule that builds up your strength. Start modestly with a climb of 1,000–1,500 feet on the first day and then gradually increase the number of feet you climb and the number of hours you walk until you can manage five to eight hours and a 3,000–6,000-foot climb.
9. Put on extra clothing when you take a break at high elevation.
10. If you're not wearing waterproof clothing, put it on when it starts to rain, before you get too wet.
11. Take care of any foot problems immediately, even during the hike, and again in the morning.
12. Take a good, deep, hot bath upon your return from each walk.

You may absolutely love Switzerland—its beauty, the grandeur of its white-capped mountains, the well-kept paths, the lifts, cable cars and trains that are so convenient in planning walks. On the other hand, you may feel that it is overly "civilized," that all the equipment set up for skiers, though useful, mars the natural beauty of the landscape in some places. (We tend to do our hiking away from the pilons and ski lifts whenever we can.) This is all a matter of personal taste. The emphasis on nature and authentic surroundings that are found in many American national and state parks may provide the kind of setting that you prefer. The next chapter will give you a picture of mountain walking in the New World.

America the Beautiful

Chapter 9

Our first trip to New Hampshire was when our daughters were quite young—nine and thirteen. We had decided to spend a week walking in the White Mountains and ordered a family room at Pinkham Notch. While there are many excellent places to use as a center for hiking in the area, Pinkham Notch is unique. It serves as a base camp for the Appalachian Mountain Club, and is within easy range of a number of classic climbs, including Mount Washington, the most famous mountain in the Presidential Range.

For newcomers to the White Mountains, this is an exciting introduction to New England walking. The place is filled with people of all ages and experience, families, groups, and individuals. A lot of mixing goes on in the big dining room, where generous helpings of nourishing food are served. Pamphlets, maps, and advice are readily available, so it is easy to find out in advance what kind of walk you can expect on any chosen trail. How long is the walk? How many hours will it take? Is it very difficult? Can I take my kids on this walk without any qualms?

Our children loved the atmosphere and threw themselves into hiking enthusiastically. It was early summer and we were lucky with the weather: not one walk was rained out. The terrain is varied and we found plenty of streams to cross, rocks to climb, natural ponds to paddle in. There were two big treats during that week. One was climbing Mount Washington, which, at 6,288 feet, is the highest mountain in northeastern United States. (The base camp at Pinkham Notch is 2,032 feet above sea level, so the actual climb was a little over 4,000 feet, a reasonable amount of walking for an experienced family, even if the kids weren't that old. It's a challenge, but by no means too much.) Driving around, you sometimes come across cars with a window sticker claiming to have climbed Mount Washington—the car that is, not the driver! While there is an auto road that cars can take up, without a doubt the best way to get to the top is by foot, up one of the trails circling the mountain and eventually lifting you to an area strewn with rocks. The excitement grows when you come across one of the famous signs of the area warning that winds of over two hundred miles per hour have been experienced there and that you should be on guard. (One of the advantages of being at Pinkham Notch is that you can get weather forecasts easily and chose your walk accordingly. The extremely high winds are rare.)

No feeling of exhilaration at reaching the top comes with sitting in a car as it chugs up. It's the challenge— walking up through deciduous forest, crossing streams, reaching the fir trees, and then above the treeline to the rocky approach to the top—it's this that gives you the high, not merely being there.

Our second treat came after the peak of Mount Washington. From there, we took the Crawford Path over to the Lakes of the Clouds, about a thousand feet lower, where we stayed overnight at the AMC hut, returning to Pinkham Notch the next day. Being at the hut was an adventure in itself: a little building at 5,000 feet, facing the elements alone, illuminated by kerosene lamps at night. The huts are kept up during the summer months by young people —often college students— who enjoy their time in the

CHARLOTTE RICKER ON CLIMBING SOUTH TWIN MOUNTAIN IN 1882

"I am well-nigh exhausted, but the scene outspread before me is of such exceeding glory and magnitude, and there is such an exultation in the thought that I, a woman, unused to privation and fatigue, have reached a height found unattainable by stalwart men because of the difficulties to be encountered by the way, I forget for the moment that I am suffering from pain and thirst and weariness."

—*Julie Boardman,* When Women and Mountains Meet

THE PRESIDENTIAL RANGE

In the Range are mountains named for such presidents as Washington, Jefferson, Monroe and Madison. Though he was never president, Franklin has a mountain too, as does Sam Adams. Among the more curious names are Jefferson's Knee, Low's Bald Spot, and Six Husbands Trail.

mountains and provide food, service, entertainment. During our stay one of the girls brought out her guitar and we all sang for a while.

When we were invited to spend the fall term at Dartmouth College recently, we were particularly enthusiastic. Not only would we enjoy working there, but Dartmouth is in Hanover, New Hampshire within easy reach of the White Mountains (as well as the Green Mountains of Vermont). With all our fond memories, we were eager to see the region again, this time in the fall. We couldn't wait to get out on the trail as soon as possible. A couple of days after arriving, we threw some things into our backpacks—waterproof clothing, compass, maps, flashlight, a snack—walked down Park Street for ten minutes, crossed the parking lot near a supermarket, and headed up the Appalachian Trail!

The famous Appalachian Trail is a footpath that runs from Maine to Georgia for 2,200 miles, following the mountains that stretch from north to south in the eastern American states. Every year many hundreds of people set out to "do" the trail, starting their odyssey in the early spring and finishing about six months later in the fall. Before leaving they have done a huge amount of preparation, reading up on the Trail, getting themselves fit, readying the gear that they will need, down to the last detail, arranging for the mailing of food parcels, so they can pick them up at post offices along the way. Only one in ten actually completes the whole trip, but everyone comes away from it with enough stories and memories to last many a winter's night. From where we were, it was about another four weeks' walking up to Mount Katahdin in Maine where the trail ends for people heading north. And October is the time for the last hikers to complete the whole route, before the snow comes, making the mountains all but impassable.

On that first day and later on other hikes, we ran into a number of people who were approaching the end of their long walk and some were happy to take a break and talk to us about it. Everyone seemed enthusiastic about their experience, in spite of the difficulties encountered. (One man had a hernia problem on the way, went to a local hospital in the south for surgery, recuperated for a few days, and set off on the Trail again!) Many of those we met were walking alone but said they tended to meet up with others wherever they stopped for the night. There were also couples, including one pair who had already done most of the Appalachian Trail a few years before, but had then run into fierce storms in the last

AMERICA THE BEAUTIFUL

month and had to stop. So they had started it all over again this year in Georgia and, when we met them, had reached their goal in Maine and were doubling back to meet some people in New Hampshire. They had even cooked all their food at home, dehydrated and then packaged it, so that they could just add water and have good home cooking during their momentous hike. And there was a young couple who had given up their jobs and had now almost finished the Appalachian Trail. He confided to me (while she was still out of sight) that after this experience he felt that they were probably going to get married—having gotten along so well throughout the arduous journey.

The stretch of Appalachian Trail starting in Hanover covers just four miles of rocky ground over to Trescott Road and the round trip made an easy afternoon's walk for us, with some climbing and occasional views. In the Hanover area we found plenty of locals out on the trail enjoying the fine weather, or walking their dogs. Women, in groups or alone, use the Appalachian and other paths in the White Mountains. But if you are not an experienced walker or don't know the trail well, it's usually best—for men or women—to do your walking in the company of someone else.

At other times that fall we picked up the AT elsewhere in the White Mountains. As it wanders all over the mountains up and down the eastern seaboard you may well be able to find a little chunk of the Trail not too far away, if you live in the east. This may give some additional excitement to your walking and you will usually find the AT very well marked with a painted white rectangle.

Walking in North America

It's impossible to generalize about a whole continent, or even about a whole country, but I'd like to point out certain contrasts between walking in the Alps and walking in New England and you can draw some broader conclusions from that. If you're used to walking in the States, you'll clearly find differences, beyond the views, from hiking in Switzerland. And if you're coming over from Europe, you will certainly find that mountain walking in America is a new experience. Why?

The Nature of the Path

While there are many different kinds of paths in American mountains it is safe to say that the ordinary path, out in the country, will be more natural, or rougher in surface than what you get in the Swiss Alps. You'll find more tree roots, more rock face and logs to contend with. It's less "civilized." This doesn't mean that you can't find wonderfully graded and surfaced paths in American parks, but you can expect that forests and mountains will have been left more in their natural state and that the walker has to pick her way as best she can. Fallen trees are often left where they are, instead of being cleared away. This is the policy in many states and the logs on the ground then become hosts to many woodland creatures large and small.

Of course, in America as in Europe, you may find steps carved into steep climbs or ropes attached to rock at a particularly slippery juncture. But you may not. Nature is often left to itself in all its primeval beauty and inaccessible glory. You may find this a nuisance at the time or you may appreciate the raw state of nature at its most authentic, but you will certainly get a sense of the original state of things.

Trail Marking

In keeping with this policy, American paths are not as conscientiously marked as those in the Swiss Alps. I have rarely had to think twice about which way to go on a Swiss path, but have often pondered over possible directions in America.

American paths are definitely marked. Each one will have its own symbol and color, usually painted well up on a tree. Just as the AT has the white rectangle, other paths will be marked with a blue rectangle, a colored dot or circle or triangle. At times you have the feeling that the person marking the trail went mad painting signs; at others you will think that he must have run out of paint. You will find that when the path changes direction there

SUGGESTION:

It's always advisable to check in with the local park rangers or other experts on particular conditions or problems if you're in a new area. For example, in Rocky Mountain National Park hikers are warned not to be above a certain altitude in the afternoon because of the danger of lightning. This is not a situation common to most places and would therefore not ordinarily be expected.

will be a double symbol—for example, two white rectangles painted on the tree—indicating that you should be looking to the left or right to see where the trail turns.

Even without the marker the path is often so clear that you don't have to be shown where it is. But it is precisely when the path is not clear for some reason—maybe it crosses bare rock or leaves or snow have filled in the forest floor—that you have to be super careful to find the next signpost. What you must avoid is getting lost.

Once in Wyoming we picked up a path that appeared to be going where we were heading. It was not marked with any symbols, but did look like a well-worn path. We descended very far down toward the river when suddenly the path petered out and ended in a kind of flattened-out circle. It was only then that we realized we'd been following an animal trail and the deer, or whatever the animals were, had simply circled round and lain down at the bottom, leaving us absolutely nowhere!

Notations on Length of Walk

There is a clear difference between Europeans and Americans on how to assess the length of a route. In the Swiss Alps, for example, there is a sign at the beginning of the path, or at the trailhead, showing your destination and the time it should take some average walker to reach it. The timing will be down to the number of minutes, as in 3½ st (three and a half hours) or even 3 hours and 20 minutes. But in America people usually talk about the distance that will be covered.

So at the beginning of a path in New Hampshire you'll see a sign indicating that your goal is four miles away. You won't be told how long it might take to get there, nor will you be told how much of a climb it is. You have to make these assessments after looking at a map with contours on it or consulting a guidebook on local walks.

It is also rare to find frequent signposting on how far you still have to go, as you'll get in the Swiss Alps. This may stem from the same philosophy mentioned before of not over-civilizing the forests and mountains and is closer to the British attitude. So you have to keep track of your own progress. If you've selected a modest route, it's not of the utmost importance to know exactly how much ground you've covered. But if you have chosen a more ambitious walk, you'll want to make sure that you reach the end of your route—and your car or bus—in daylight.

For this reason you often run into people in American mountains who use a pedometer to keep track of distance covered. While a pedometer is not necessary, many hikers like to see how far they've gone, whether they're in the mountains or just checking on their daily walking or jogging routine.

In the same vein, hikers frequently use an altimeter in less well-marked areas.

Hikers On Your Path

Whether you are in the Alps or the White Mountains, the Dolomites or the Rockies, you will find in general that hikers are a friendly group. It is usual to greet people approaching you with a "hello" or "hi". Chance meetings are often interesting and other hikers are generally glad to be helpful if you want to find your position on the map or ask how far it is to the top.

USING A PEDOMETER:

- *You can buy a pedometer in most sports stores.*
- *This mechanical gadget is based upon the length of your average stride, so to make it work, you have to adjust the pedometer to the distance between your feet when you are walking normally.*
- *Once adjusted, it can be used easily, hung at the belt.*
- *Knowing the distance you have walked is useful if you know how long the path is. Then you can work out how far you have to go.*

USING A ALTIMETER:

This is very useful if you want to know just where you are, but it depends upon your being able to coordinate what height you are at with the contours on the map. The altimeter has to be pre-set to the starting altitude. By using it you can establish how high you are and what part of the path that puts you on. While not necessary for most marked paths, it's another useful tool for giving you an idea of where you are, particularly if there are few signs along the way.

AMERICA THE BEAUTIFUL

Planning a Stay in New Hampshire

While this section deals with New Hampshire, it can be read as a general pattern for planning a visit to any mountain region in the United States and presents some of the considerations to take into account.

When?

The question of when you should take your vacation clearly depends upon your own schedule, but keep in mind that good mountain walking, especially for beginners, should not be done in the winter. Spring in New England can be very wet and muddy, thus leaving us with **summer and early fall, two wonderful walking seasons**. (In other parts of America, springtime can be a perfect time for the mountains.)

Summer has clear advantages from a few points of view. The days are very long, giving you a maximum amount of walking time. Up in the mountains, in the northeast, intense heat should not be too much of a problem. The forests give plenty of shade. The mountain top is not as cold as in other seasons. Coming back down in the cooler afternoons is pleasant. Don't forget, though, that part of the summer can be black fly season, so come equipped. These are swarms of stinging insects and, whether a region has mosquitoes, midges, black fly or anything similar, bring some kind of repellant with you to avoid being on a collision course with them.

"There is a sumptuous variety about the New England weather that compels the stranger's admiration—and regret. . . . But it gets through more business in Spring than in any other season. In the Spring I have counted one hundred and thirty-six different kinds of weather inside of twenty-four hours."

—*Mark Twain, 1876*

Experienced walkers and doctors seem agreed that a repellant known as DEET is the most effective against biting insects generally, though they also agree that it's best not to put in direct contact with the skin. So the best advice is to apply it to your clothing—cuffs, hat, neckline—to protect you without causing any personal harm. Black flies, though, are very hard to deal with effectively. I can only say that walking in the northeast in the autumn I have not encountered them.

The autumn has a character of its own and the walker in the White Mountains in late September or October is offered a vivid show of color that is unrivaled. This is a tremendous bonus. The forest floor is soft and pleasant to the foot. Ferns and rich undergrowth abound. Toward the end of the fall there is such an abundance of dry colored leaves that it can be hard to see the path. A sibilant rustle of fallen leaves accompanies you as you walk. True, it is dark by six, but you still have a reasonable number of daylight hours in which to enjoy Nature's greatest show. Except on the weekends, most of the paths are almost deserted and you can feel that you have the mountain to yourself.

> *"Leaves, like the things of man, you*
> *With your fresh thoughts care for, can you?*
> *Ah! as the heart grows older*
> *It will come to such sights colder*
> *By and by, nor spare a sigh*
> *Though worlds of wanwood leafmeal lie;*
> *And yet you will weep and know why."*
> *—Gerard Manley Hopkins*

Picking a Center

Central and northern New Hampshire are filled with rich forests, impressive mountains and broad panoramas. You can readily find an excellent center to use as your home base, taking different walks up into the mountains every day. A little reading will give you plenty of ideas about the right place for you to stay, depending on your transportation needs, whether you are traveling with family or friends, how many other activities you are looking for in the same area and the level of comfort you seek.

If you are attracted by the bustling mountain atmosphere of Pinkham Notch, that would be a natural choice, as so many good walks can be started right in the area or an easy drive away. Shuttle buses are available during the season so that hikers can get to and from paths a little further afield without having to use a car of their own. For beginners it makes sense to start in a place where information and advice are readily available.

But good hiking centers abound and you might want to choose one of the others, or divide your time between two. You could, for example, stay away from the higher mountains and decide to spend a few days in the Hanover area, right on the Vermont border. As the home of the famous Dartmouth College, the town of Hanover (population about 4,000) is very charming, with a picturesque Main Street, restaurants, shops for picking up the makings for lunch, and good sports equipment stores in the neighborhood. It also offers a few rainy day activities in the event of inclement weather.

> *"The Vermont mountains stretch*
> *extending straight;*
> *New Hampshire mountains curl up*
> *in a coil."*
> —Robert Frost

Let's use this for a sample run. You have arrived in Hanover, or one of the nearby towns (Woodstock, Vermont or White River Junction, New Hampshire, for example) and you want to plan a few days in the local mountains.

How To Start?

Once you arrive, you should sit down and **consult the local maps and any hiking guidebooks that you have**. You may have already done this at home, before leaving. If at all possible, it is helpful to have your maps before you get to the area. This isn't always easy, but either in a fine map or sporting goods store, or through the Internet, maps and guidebooks can be bought in advance. Otherwise, buying local surveyor's maps, with trails clearly marked, should be your first priority upon arrival.

Besides the maps and books, you may also want to consult local people—your hosts, your hotel, the park rangers office or, in the case of Hanover, the Dartmouth Outing Club, located on the Green.

PREPARATION:

During those long winter nights you can be doing research in preparation for next summer's walking. Get in touch by mail, phone, Internet, with the Appalachian Mountain Club or the Sierra Club or the headquarters of the specific state or national park that you will be visiting. Get as much information from them as you can about the terrain, trails, local facilities, organized activities or anything else that you want to know.

Locate mountains in the area and then check with the guidebook about walks, or vice versa. How high is the mountain? How long will the walk take? It is not always easy to judge length of time from a guidebook, because you don't know their standards. Their "average walker" may do the hike much faster (or slower) than you and it is only after you have worked with a book for a while that you can assess your own speed in comparison with that of the author. So allow yourself extra time to do the roundtrip in the beginning, leaving plenty of margin for error.

Judging how long it will take. No single criterion is enough to assess the difficulty of a walk. In a way, the easiest is the Swiss system: find out *how much time* a walk should take. That is very straightforward. But the time that it takes me to complete a certain route could be longer or shorter than the time that it takes you. We were once shocked in Grindelwald, in the Swiss Bernese Oberland, when we returned after a year or so and found that the signs had been re-done and all the times for walks had been shortened! Someone must have decided that the previous times had been too long, but this wasn't the case for us. In the beginning, we thought that we were just out of shape, until we realized what had happened.

Knowing *how many miles* are in a walk can be very useful, but it is not enough in itself. Clearly, four miles along a flat, clean path will take

WHAT TO GET FROM A HIKING GUIDEBOOK:

1. *Read the descriptions of possible walks.*
2. *Check the number of miles and height to be climbed.*
3. *Assess the difficulty of the walk from the description. Does it mention any tricky ascents or descents? Is the route exceptionally long or inadequately marked?*
4. *Using all the given facts provided in the guidebook, select some particularly attractive and suitable walks.*
5. *The guidebook should serve as a reference tool. Once you have started using it—or a combination of a couple of guidebooks—you will be able to estimate the reliability of the descriptions.*

much less time than four miles on a steep path with roots and boulders under foot. Four miles walked fast down a city street takes an hour. But three miles in the Himalayas once took us a very long day.

You have to know *how much altitude* you will be climbing as well. In the Alps I ordinarily reckon three quarters of an hour to an hour per thousand feet, but this calculation doesn't work as neatly in the White Mountains. These are older mountains and are more spread out, so you are covering far more territory in ascending a mountain in New Hampshire and that takes more time.

By combining everything you know about a given walk you'll be able to plan accordingly. You'll become quite expert at this very soon. The main thing is to be as well informed as possible and to leave yourself plenty of time.

Good Beginning Options

If you are an absolute beginner or not in good form, start with a truly easy climb. Probably the least demanding hike in the area would be Mount Tom (also known as Tom's Mount) in Woodstock, just over in Vermont. It's really almost too low for the purpose.

The height of the climb is only about 500 feet. The distance of the walk is listed as about a mile and a half and the only reason that it could be that long is that the trail ascends in a very gentle way, with long zigzags (called switchbacks in New England) back and forth up the little mountain. The ascent is so gradual that you can hardly tell that you are going uphill at all, with only the last one hundred yards providing a real climb. Indeed, if you are impatient with the long swings, feel free to take the little shortcuts connecting level to level. Even they aren't too demanding.

The walk itself is beautiful, just on the edge of the center of Woodstock, Vermont. The woods are dense and once at the top—especially if you are doing this when there are no leaves on the trees—you look down on the incredibly picturesque little town, which is just below. Within view as well are rivers and rolling countryside. This is a perfect first mountain, as gentle as can be. If you want to make a day of it, continue on the path beyond the top as far as you care to, before turning back.

A popular walk in the Hanover area also makes a perfect beginning—or second day—climb. This is Cardigan, a classic 1,000-foot mountain, which is a little over two miles round trip. This is the complete mountain experience: it includes beautiful woods, good elevation, a walk across stone slabs at the top and fine views in all directions. And, without adding much to the distance, you can also make it a circular trip instead of following the same path down. If at all possible, we usually choose to make some kind of loop instead of returning by the same route.

The path up Cardigan is very well marked. Like many New England mountains it is crowned at the top with stone. It is worthwhile to get experience in walking up and down stone. If your boots have good soles—and they should—you can walk straight down on dry stone, whatever the angle, without fear of falling. *Trust your boots.* But if the stone is wet and slippery, care has to be taken in traversing it. Experience will be your best teacher.

TRAILHEADS:
Use your trail map to locate the trailhead, or the place where your path begins. On some maps this is indicated by a P for the parking space that is near the start of the trail. On other maps you will just have to see where the road you will be driving on meets the path. In many a mountain village a good number of trails can be reached within an easy stroll of where you are staying.

WALKING DOWNHILL
Walking downhill requires a greater variety of skills than climbing up and it's important to master those skills—otherwise, you can waste time. *You will want to adapt your method of descent to the terrain:*

- *A good path and easy grading*—select your own speed. There's nothing more pleasant than strolling down a mountain in the late afternoon, after a day's hard climb, enjoying the scenery, some desultory conversation and the thought of the bath and dinner ahead. But you can also easily hurry if you need to.

- If there's *a good path and a fairly steep gradient*, you might choose to go fast, gliding down, with knees bent and slightly bowlegged, allowing gravity to do the work. With experience you can descend two or even three thousand feet in an hour this way.

AMERICA THE BEAUTIFUL

- *On a wide very steep slope of grass or rock*—where there's no clear path—you will often find it easier to zigzag down in order to spare excessive wear on knees and toes.
- *On narrow sections of dry and steep rock*, walk straight down, trusting your boots; you won't slip as long as you keep upright. Don't lean back.
- *On wet rock*, be ultra-careful, descending cautiously. Use your sticks here or nearby branches or other handholds. Go down on your rear end if necessary.
- *On snow or mud*, dig in your heels as you march down; you'll probably find this effective in descending gulleys of loose rock and stones, too. At times, this means a snail's pace; at others, a very rapid descent as you make a constant succession of slides, using first one foot then the other, trailing snow or a shower of stones behind you.

Moderate Climbs

There are many excellent choices for walks that will take you up a few thousand feet, with a roundtrip time of several hours. One example in the Hanover/Woodstock area is Moosilauke. This is a mountain actually owned by Dartmouth College (with an old wooden recreation center at its base) which is very popular not only among students, but for local walkers of all ages. Like so many fine mountains in the region, it offers an attractive combination of varying terrain, vegetation, challenges and views. The first part of the hike takes you through deciduous forest, crossing little bridges over streams from time to time. Later, you can join what is called a carriage road—a broad path wide enough to accommodate the horse-drawn carriages that used to take passengers up to the top of Moosilauke. Today you can only reach the windy summit on foot. Weather permitting, there are excellent views toward the Presidential Range from there. Like Cardigan, the trees become fir and eventually, above the tree line, there is rock at the top. There are fine options for round trips back to the lodge.

Getting onto the Appalachian Trail where it can be picked up inside Hanover is also an excellent way to get your mountain legs. Or if you're in the Woodstock area, you can pick up the AT there for a bit.

Somewhat further afield is another excellent climb, an eight-mile roundtrip walk 3,000 feet up Mount Liberty, with an exciting summit reached by a narrow stone traverse, and breathtaking views over the White Mountains and the New Hampshire countryside. When we got to the top, it was very windy, but I was not going to be done out of the lunch that I had so lovingly packed hours before. So we found a protected spot, sheltered by a projecting rock, and enjoyed our food and the view for a while before making our way down.

Not far from here is the Flume area which itself is an attractive center for mountain walking. For an easy climb, try Mount Pemigawasett, which is a little over a thousand feet in elevation and makes up a three-mile roundtrip. There

PACK IN, PACK OUT:
Everyone brings water and food with them when they are hiking. The principle is "Pack in; pack out." Whatever you carry into the mountains should go out again in your backpack. It's only in this way that the woods stay as clean and free from litter as they do.

are excellent views from the top, in all directions. One advantage of walking here is that this climb, and some others, are near the Flume Visitor Center, where you can not only pick up information and food, but also find lavatories.

Toilets

Begin with the premise that there are usually none, although there are exceptions. In various national parks you will find toilets, even in some quite surprising places. In Glacier National Park in Montana and in the Grand Tetons in Wyoming I have, gratefully, come across lavatories. In Switzerland, most walks end at a little restaurant or inn—and a restroom.

But you have to be prepared, if you can't hold out for hours, to use the woods as your toilet, squatting in an out-of-the-way place.

On many many walks you will have some regret that, at least in this concern, you were not born a man. It's so much easier for them. The woods were made for males to pee behind every tree and bush. Women have to squat, ungainly though it seems. Just make sure that you find a discreet place, that you have toilet paper with you and can bury it safely. There are more complications if you are having your period but you can cope even with this if you come well prepared. A plastic bag for carrying out will serve the purpose till you get back to your hotel room or hostel. One main concern, which we all share, is that the beautiful woodlands and mountainsides are not littered with toilet paper and other unpleasant reminders of the walkers' invasion.

You may be able to limit stops to urinate by avoiding excessive coffee, tea, or chocolate, or anything else (such as alcohol) that is diuretic in nature. Diuretics also dehydrate you, causing another problem. Don't keep yourself from drinking when you need fluid. In the morning you may want to have herbal tea or a coffee substitute (or decaf) instead of your usual beverage. These will not cause the same problems. Do not under any circumstances try to hold out for a long time because you want to avoid the whole experience. You should relieve yourself when necessary.

Make sure that you use a toilet just before starting on your hike, even if it means stopping at a gas station en route to the trailhead.

Various people have written on the problem that women have relieving themselves in the great outdoors. I have seen amazing and inventive ideas of particular ways to stand or crouch; some writers suggest carrying a small trowel for covering up, and so on. But for day-hiking, I'd stick to the discreet but natural use of the woods without too much innovative acrobatics.

Your Period

Unless you have severe problems during your period there is no reason that you should curtail your mountain activities, certainly not in day-walks. There is one thing, however, that you should be careful about: do not leave a tampon in for more than six hours, as there is a danger of infection. Wherever you are, it is important to change tampons, regardless of whether or not there's a toilet around.

If you are walking in high mountains for two weeks or more and you have your period, it is advisable to take an iron supplement. You're losing blood and hemoglobin—the compound that carries oxygen in the blood—drops during menstruation. The iron will allow your body to replenish its hemoglobin. (This doesn't apply to day-walking in moderately high mountains.)

If you're on the pill and feel that you'd really rather not have your period just when you're taking off a week to walk in the mountains, contact your doctor a couple of weeks before your vacation. She will be able to help you adjust your schedule so as to avoid the inconvenience.

A last caveat about your period. It's inadvisable to do walking in grizzly bear country during a time that the smell of blood could arouse the bear's interest. As grizzlies are only in very specific places—in the northern Rockies, for instance—this warning is of limited application.

If You Are Pregnant

There are no definitive research-based guidelines for activity during pregnancy. Pregnant women certainly should not go hiking at high altitudes, that is, over 8,000 feet. In general, the accepted wisdom is that pregnant women shouldn't exercise vigorously for more than forty-five minutes a day at any time during pregnancy. The definition of vigorous varies with each person. How much exercise do you normally do? You may ordinarily follow a very active routine of exercise and will continue, within reason, without feeling that it is too strenuous. Researchers point out a variety of problems connected with pregnancy—from a loss of good balance with the growth of the fetus to a fear of oxygen deprivation—which cause them to be particularly cautious. If you have questions about this, ask your doctor.

Are You Ready for a Little More Adventure?

Every hike in the mountains is an adventure in itself, even if you have done a particular walk before. You may be doing it in a different season; conditions change; the weather could be different; you're walking with other people. So each day out provides a feeling of discovery. There are also other options that you can try which will add a little more adventure to your walking.

For example, in the White Mountains there is a string of huts, eight of them, where you can stay overnight. These are located high up along a section of the Appalachian Trail. Among them is the Lakes of the Clouds Hut that I mentioned earlier. These huts are so placed that each one is a day's hike from the other. So theoretically you could spend a full week a few thousand feet up, walking from hut to hut and never coming down to "civilization." The huts, run by the AMC, have shared accommodation and bathrooms (cold running water!), but are well run, clean, and they serve meals, so you don't have to worry about carrying additional food with you. They are only accessible by foot, so you will never run into people who just hopped out of a car, fresh as a daisy after you have spent the day getting there. Some are quite easy to reach (for example, Lonesome Lake Hut) and would be good for beginning walks or family hikes. Others are more strenuous (such as the Lakes of the Clouds Hut and Madison Spring Hut), but not at all out of reach once you have some uphill walking experience behind you. Of course, you don't have to do all of them in a row. You

USEFUL AMC CONTACTS:
Huts & lodges:
603-466-2727
General information:
617-523-0655, Ext. 341
www.outdoors.org

can pick one or two or more and work out a round trip hike of a few days. This is an attractive option for people looking for a little more in their vacation. Needless to say, these huts are popular and places have to be reserved many months in advance.

How to avoid getting lost. One thing that I often do if I don't see a marker ahead of me is to turn around and look back at the path I have just come along, to see if there are any symbols on the trees for people coming from the direction where I'm heading. That will at least assure me that I am on the right path.

Keep track of when you last saw a trail sign. If it seems like a long time, stop and look around, check for signs.

Don't keep going indefinitely along a path without knowing that you are on the right one. If you are not sure how to proceed (let's say that you know you've been walking on your path but it suddenly seems to have faded out ahead), then if you are with another person, one of you should stay still on the path and the other can venture ahead until you catch sight of the next sign. Then join up again and carry on.

You can't do what Hansel and Gretel did, dropping pebbles or breadcrumbs to keep track of the right path, but you can make sure that you keep careful note of where you are and avoid getting off the marked route. One thing to keep in mind: you can't simply trust your instinct. Having a good sense of direction is useful, but once you've made a number of turns in a forest and there are no landmarks because the trees block out the view you can easily get disoriented. In this case, the best thing is to rely on the markings on your path and not just a sixth sense.

AVOID GETTING LOST
- **Don't go too far without seeing a trail marker**
- **Stop and look around immediately if you feel you have lost the marked path.**
- **Check your bearings on your map and on the ground. Can you see what direction you're heading?**
- **Turn around and look back at the way you've come: can you see trail markings on trees in the other direction?**
- **If you are not alone, one person should move ahead to check the way in front while the others remain on what they think is the path.**
- **Try to re-trace your walk until you come back to the marked trail, then carefully check which way you should proceed.**

American Mountains

Luckily, North America is rich in mountain regions. There are so many magnificent areas, literally from sea to shining sea, that

AMERICA THE BEAUTIFUL

you can spend the next few decades sampling the mountains of America. Almost anywhere you live, there is something to climb nearby, perhaps in a state park, maybe in a national park, or just the local mountain down the road from your home. Many people have grown up rambling over the hills in their neighborhood. If you haven't, find out where the closest climb is and head there one weekend morning.

Out West

If you are looking for something spectacular, there is no shortage. In the west are the dramatic Rockies, which were such a barricade to early settlers heading toward the coast. Excellent walking can be had throughout the great north-south divide. Like the Appalachian Trail that runs from Maine to Georgia in the Eastern states, the Continental Divide Trail stretches over thousands of miles, in this case from the Montana border with Canada in the north to the Mexican border in the south. You can pick up some portion of the Trail and enjoy classic walking in the Rockies for a day or a week or more.

LOOKING FOR ANIMALS?

If you'd like the added pleasure of seeing animals in their natural habitat while doing your mountain walking, try Grand Teton National Park in Wyoming. Encounters with moose, elk, bears, and a variety of other animals and birds make this area a paradise for nature lovers. Far from traffic these animals can be encountered in their own natural surroundings.

***** ***** ***** *****

Or, try the mountains of northern Georgia in Chattahoochee National Forest where hundreds of species find shelter: deer, raccoons, turkeys, black bears. If you're lucky, maybe you'll see some of them!

In California you can walk in the magnificent Sierra Nevada, one of the longest mountain ranges in the world, stretching 400 miles, with over a dozen 14,000-foot peaks. With the snowcapped Cascades, the Sequoia National Park, and Yosemite National Park—a place of unparalleled natural beauty—the region offers boundless opportunities for hiking and backpacking. Visitor Centers provide all the information you will need for your walks. Other classic walks can be joined if you hook up with some part of the Pacific Crest National Scenic Trail, which swings down from the State of Washington to southern California. This trail together with the Continental Divide Trail and the Appalachian Trail is one of the three main long-distance mountain routes of the United States, covering vast territory and offering the walker the best of long-distance hiking.

In the state of Washington stands Mount Rainier, a 14,410-foot volcanic mountain with a glacier at the top and rain forest at its base. Nearly all of the national park surrounding it has been preserved as wilderness. Here again you can find lodging and information through the visitor centers. In many national parks there are organized hikes for people who prefer walking in groups, bird watching, and other forms of guiding.

In the Southwest

The Grand Canyon is a special case. It may not be a mountain, but it involves a climb, in reverse. Walking here is something truly out of the ordinary. The entire panorama, the deep canyon descending over a mile down, the river at the bottom: all this brings home a feeling of the creation of the earth's surface during a time of monumental chaos.

In planning your day's walk, you have to be particularly careful precisely because you start out on a descent and return by walking uphill. In the ordinary hike, the walker expends a lot of effort on the climb in the first half of the day and then just has the descent toward the end. In this case, you'll find yourself strolling down a pleasant path—that is, the easier part—and then having to climb every last inch to get back. So be careful to allow plenty of time and energy for returning to your starting point.

I remember walking down to an inviting point one February a few years ago, only to realize that we were thousands of feet below our starting point and they would all have to be walked back up before nightfall. This was complicated by the existence of a winter snowfield for about a mile and a half, toward the top of the walk. It didn't pose a problem because we had rented crampons from a local shop and just had to put them on at the start of the snow field and take them off when we reached dry ground. (Crampons are the best thing to use on steep snow or ice because they add even more traction to the soles of your boots.) But on our return, Leora, her husband, and I were working hard to get to the top before the last light had left the sky, and putting on the crampons took up more time than we could spare. We were also very worried about another couple we had passed, much further down. The woman was wearing ordinary shoes with little heels and neither seemed to be very good walkers. How they crossed the snowfield and what time they reached the top is something we don't know, though we phoned the park rangers to alert them to the problem.

The Southeast

It would be impossible to review here all the various mountain opportunities that enrich North America. Extending into the southeast are the Appalachians, some

There is an astounding array of national parks in America. To get an idea of what each one has to offer, either write to a few information centers, or use the Internet. Here's the official National Park Service site: http://www.nps.gov

of the oldest mountains on earth (just as the Sierra Nevada is one of the youngest ranges). With their exquisite combination of deep forest, flowering magnolia, streams, and waterfalls, they offer extraordinary scenery to the walker. Take some long hikes there in the spring or summer and drink in the beauty that is only accessible when you traverse on foot.

The Northeast
In New York State are the Catskills within easy reach of New York City and the more rugged Adirondacks further to the north. The Appalachian Trail makes its way up through the state. And of course New England has the rocky and wild White Mountains of New Hampshire and the softer, rounder Green Mountains of Vermont.

And Way to the North . . .
The stupendous mountains of Alaska hold a rugged attraction of their own, filled with game of all kinds and towering in the coldest and northern-most state of the Union. The highest mountain in the United States is situated in Denali National Park—Mount McKinley, all 20,320 feet of it. Come between June and September and enjoy great backcountry hiking and some of the most magnificent mountains in the hemisphere.

This is an extraordinarily brief sweep of the potential areas that you can visit for mountain walking. There are

Mountaineers love to set goals for themselves and even walkers who are ascending without the use of pitons and ropes like to "collect" mountains. For instance, in the White Mountains of New Hampshire walkers who spend a lot of time there check off the 4,000-foot mountains that they have climbed, hoping to do them all—there are 48. In the English Lake District, which is somewhat lower, there is a cult of "collecting" 3,000-foot peaks. In Switzerland, of course, it's meters and not feet and climbers are counting the number of 4,000-meter (12,000–13,000-foot) peaks they've conquered. But those are mainly mountains that require rock or ice climbing techniques.

so many hidden areas just waiting to be explored. Only recently a survey team completed a several-years sweep of backwoods areas within

Yellowstone National Park. Who would have believed that the group discovered dozens of streams and waterfalls in this extremely popular park that had never been registered on the local maps? Whether you are visiting well-trodden paths up a mountain a few miles from your hometown or hiking along a backwoods path far from the tourist track, the particular walk you take will be full of discovery for you.

More Notes on Walking

In summing up some of the experiences you will have in walking the mountains of America, let's take in a few more details and pointers about the art of uphill hiking.

- **Make your walk circular,** so that you can return by a somewhat different path and you will get in additional views and a more varied route. Sit down with your map and work out good roundtrips whenever it seems feasible, making sure that you end up where you left your car, or near enough. We recently did this to make our walk more "interesting" and ended up miles down the road from where we'd parked out car. We didn't mind, but remember that this extra walking will come at the end of a long day's excursion.

- If you are walking with other people and you have two cars at your disposal, another excellent option is to **leave one car at the place where you will end your walk and then all drive to the trailhead in the other car,** so that you don't have to come back the way you ascended. In this way, for example, you can string out a hike along the Appalachian Trail or any other lineal path and see twice as much in each day's walk.

- Because American trails can be more "natural" and less developed, **you might enjoy your mountain walking even better with a walking stick**. Some people simply use ski poles. But you can buy good walking sticks in sports supply stores, either individual ones or in pairs, depending on your preference. A stick can be particularly useful descending steep ground or in dealing with a slippery patch. Lots of hikers, young and old, enjoy using them. I tend to make use of a walking stick in the U.S. (or in the Himalayas) more often than I do in the Swiss Alps.

- Anywhere, whether you are in New England or in Colorado, in the English Lake District or in the Blue Ridge Mountains, you should **check on the local weather before you set out**. Some climbing centers have a barometer hanging in the window; if not your hotel should have the latest weather forecast. In many places, we go walking whatever the weather. (If you waited for good dry weather in some parts of Britain, for example, you'd have a very long wait!) But mountain storms can be fierce and lightning can be dangerous, so knowing what to expect from the weather can help you decide if this is a day when you'll do something else. Indeed, if you see a serious storm brewing in the mountains, it's good policy to curtail your walk and head for home. You certainly do not want to be caught in the mountains in the snow, where the trail can be covered over.

- **Bring a flashlight!** When you leave on a bright morning you don't think that it's worth carrying, but at 5:30 on an autumn afternoon in Maine and still on the path, you'll feel reassured, with your flashlight in a pocket of your backpack. A friend of ours was descending Mount Liberty in the White Mountains and passed a small party making their way up. It was afternoon and he was concerned that they might end up coming down in the dark, so, after worrying about it for a while, he left his flashlight for them in a conspicuous place where they'd find it on the way down.

- In North America there is a wealth of animals that you might see in your meanderings. This is one of the terrific attractions of walking in the New World. Although I have only come upon them as they are crossing the road, there are large numbers of deer, moose, and some bears, living in the New England forests. Out West the variety of wildlife is astonishing—from mountain goats to all kinds of bears (including grizzlies in some areas!) to moose, elk, and birds of every description. Most of the time the nearness of these animals adds immeasurably to your hiking, though some are potentially dangerous. Check your area before setting out. In Glacier National Park, for example, signs in the woods warn you of local grizzly bears. You can get advice on the spot on how to deal with the potential problem of a nearby grizzly bear—anything from wearing bells around your neck, to keeping up a lively chatter to warn off any bears within hearing distance. The theory is that these bears are just as anxious to avoid you as you are to keep away from them—but they can be deadly if confronted. In grizzly country, you might feel more comfortable joining one of the groups organized by the parks service, or at least consulting a park ranger.

- If you choose to go walking in the late fall, **check on the dates of the hunting season**. We found in New Hampshire, for instance, that almost every mountain in the state is open to hunting during a large part of November and early December. You really do not want to be walking in the woods when hunters are liable to shoot anything that is moving. Some walkers wear bright orange jackets and go into the woods anyway, but this may not be everybody's cup of tea.

Finally, remember to **reserve a place to stay in the mountains as early as possible,** particularly if you are heading for a popular region. While you may always find a room somewhere, certain places—like Pinkham Notch in New Hampshire or some of the hotel spaces within Grand Teton National Park or Yosemite—will be booked early. The accommodations in many national parks can often be charming, comfortable, and affordable, which means that plenty of people want to stay there. So plan ahead, make your reservations, and prepare yourself for the vacation of a lifetime!

Walking in the English Lake District

Chapter 10

Every mountain range presents its own characteristics and its own challenges. These variations are a function of the kind of terrain, the age (and shape) of the mountains, and the weather. Just as alpine hiking contrasts with a walk in the New Hampshire woods, so we can now see a third variant: walking in the English Lake District.

The mountains of the Lake District are in northwest England, just south of the Scottish border. While they are the highest mountains inside England, compared to the Alps or the Rockies, they are much older and lower. The Cumberland mountains were formed about four hundred million years ago in the Palaeozoic period, like those of Scotland, Ireland, and Scandinavia. They are characterized by gently rounded shapes. Nowhere do they reach even 4,000 feet. Though they are older and lower, the area is wild and unspoiled, lonely and "uncivilized," and wandering through the Lake District, crossing from mountain to mountain, the walker feels very far from the hustle and bustle of the twenty-first century.

The variety within the region of Cumbria is one of its attractions. From the cozy slopes near Grasmere with its moss-covered walls and charming stiles to the rich, green Borrowdale area, flowing with sparkling streams, to the wild, dour grandeur of Wasdale crowned with rugged peaks, the Lake District encompasses a realm of beauty and challenge.

BEST KNOWN PEAKS OF THE LAKE DISTRICT:
Great Gable
Scafell
Helvellyn
Skiddaw

Lake District Walking

Even if you've already walked the mountain trails and paths elsewhere, you'll be surprised by "the Lakes" (as the region is called). What will you find?

- SIGNPOSTING. The British tend toward even less intrusion into the landscape than the Americans. You will not be told at the beginning of a walk how far you are going (or how long it will take). Often you will not be told where the path leads. There are sometimes indicators at trailheads and after that you can walk for hours on your path without seeing any other sign.

- TRAIL MARKERS. Alpine walks, as we have seen, have frequent signposts and American paths are usually marked by splashes of paint on trees or a blaze. These are uncommon in the Lake District. Much more usual are cairns, pyramid-shaped piles of stones that can suddenly appear on a vague part of the path or that are placed at regular intervals in areas where an actual path isn't clear. Sometimes, groping your way through a fog, you will, with great relief, see a large cairn looming ahead and know that you are still going in the right direction.

  > **CAIRNS**
  > *These piles of stones are found all over in the mountains—a practical way of showing the trail, particularly in areas above the tree line or where it is impossible to see an actual path. Many a time, in doubt about the direction, I have suddenly spotted a cairn off in the distance and, in gratitude, added a rock to the pile when I reached it.*

- DESCENDING INTO THE VALLEY. The Lake District is crisscrossed with paths leading over mountains and into other valleys. Because of their shapes, you can reach the top of a mountain and see a choice of paths at the summit. One will take you down to your planned destination and another will lead to quite another valley. Remember, there may not be a signpost. People do make mistakes and it's important to check your bearings carefully at the top before choosing your descent. The problem is intensified by the frequent misty weather in the Lake District: part of its charm and part of its difficulty.

You may not even see where you are going when you're at the top. That's why *it is important to have a good map on you as well as a compass.* By using both, you should be able to work out the right way down. This isn't a problem on every mountain in Cumbria, but it is definitely a Lake District phenomenon. Of course, if you're climbing a mountain and then returning to your starting point, you don't have to worry about this.

WHISTLES:
It's a good idea for each person in the group to bring a whistle if you think you'll encounter mist. This is one way to keep track of where everyone is— especially the kids.

On a recent visit to the Lake District, we reached the top of Helvellyn, one of the most beloved goals for Lake District walkers, in total cloud. We couldn't see thirty feet ahead. Worried about finding the path down to Glenridding, we asked a local man who had just made the climb up from there. Oh, he said, "just drop off the edge there." Horrified, with the literal thought of doing just that, I asked him to show us exactly the spot where we should "drop off," which he did. He then disappeared down and was soon out of sight, as we slowly dealt with the steeply curving path and scree.

Scenic Differences

- The **gentle English landscape** is characteristic of parts of the Lake District. A usual path will take the walker past ancient dry walls whose texture is witness to the vicissitudes of time and weather. These stones, laid one on another by sheep farmers hundreds of years ago to demarcate their fields, are overlaid with moss and small plants. Often growing nearby are bright pink and purple foxgloves, standing knee-high. Dark green fern-leaved bracken fills in the background, turning yellow in the fall. In many places heather gives a magical purple or pink softness to fields and marshes.

- **Gates and stiles.** As many fields are enclosed by walls, the walker has to cross from field to field in numerous inventive ways. These often add to the fun of the walk. First, of course, there may be an ordinary gate. Always remember to close the gate securely after you so that livestock can't move from one field to the next. There are also cattle-gates, semicircular gateways that you enter and then push the barrier partly around so that only a human being and not a cow can get around it. Stiles are ingenious in their variety. The most normal are stiles in the shape of a fixed ladder leaning against each side of the wall to be mounted. Just climb up one side and down the other. Other versions include individual stones jutting out from the wall, on a rising angle, with perhaps a nearby pole to hang onto. Just use them as steps and then down the other side.

". . . Among the rocks
He went, and still looked up to sun
*   and cloud,*
And listened to the wind; and, as
*   before,*
Performed all kinds of labour for
*   his sheep,*
And for the land, his small
*   inheritance.*
And to that hollow dell from time
*   to time*
Did he repair, to build the Fold of
*   which His flock had need."*
*   —William Wordsworth*

"You ask, in God's name, why I did not return when I saw the state of the weather? The true reason is simple, tho' it may be somewhat strange—the thought never once entered my head. The cause of this I suppose to be, that (I do not remember it at least) I never once in my whole life turned back in fear of the weather. Prudence is a plant, of which I, no doubt, possess some valuable specimens—but they are always in my hot-house, never out of the glasses—& least of all things would endure the climate of the mountains. In simple earnest, I never find myself alone within the embracement of rocks & hills, a traveler up an alpine road, but my spirit courses, drives, and eddies, like a Leaf in Autumn: a wild activity, of thoughts, imaginations, feelings, and impulses of motion, rises up from within me—a sort of bottom-wind, that blows to no point of the compass, & comes from I know not whence, but agitates the whole of me; my whole Being is filled with waves, as it were, that roll & stumble, one this way, & one that way, like things that have no common master. . . . The farther I ascend from animated Nature, from men, and cattle, & the common birds of the woods, & fields, the greater becomes in me the Intensity of the feeling of Life; Life seems to me then a universal spirit, that neither has, nor can have, an opposite. God is every where."

—Samuel Taylor Coleridge, January 14, 1803

- **"Wildlife."** I have personally never seen wild animals in the Lake District, though there are signs of animal burrows. What you can see—and this is quite lovely and fascinating—are sheep. Walkers come across the stone buildings and pens connected with sheep herding and sheep shearing. They also meet up with sheep, shepherds and sheep dogs on occasion and it is a great treat if you are lucky enough to run into them out in the hills. Watching the interaction of the shepherd, his dog, and his flock—the man whistling or calling his commands, the border collie rushing at the sheep and directing their progress—could fascinate the viewer for hours.
- **Water.** Of course, this is the Lake District and there are plenty of lakes to see, from the serene lakes of Buttermere to the dark and deep Wast Water, the deepest lake in England. Many walks

start and end at a lake. The lakes are not the only water. Throughout the mountains the walker encounters countless streams, falls, and small lakes high up in the mountains that are locally called tarns. This mix of mountains and water gives the district its special character.

- **Villages.** Leaving the wilds of the mountain areas, the hiker ends the day in one of the many villages found in the valleys. These are authentic villages, not just tourist spots, and are a delight to walk through. Local pubs are always fun and the bakery can provide fresh rolls for your backpack in the morning (not to speak of scones for afternoon tea!).

Two Styles of Walking in the Lake District

There are two ways to organize what the British would call a walking holiday in Cumbria. You can choose a center (as in the previous chapters) and make roundtrip walks from there. Or you can back-pack.

1. **Choosing a center.** There are dozens of delightful places to choose in the Lake District, from the large and well-known resorts of Windermere and Ambleside to tiny dots on the map, such as Buttermere or Boot. The advantage of settling on one place is that you can familiarize yourself with a single snug area, feel comfortable coming "home" each evening to the same place and sleep in the same bed every night. In many of these centers there are so many local paths that you can keep yourself busy with enjoyable walks without using a car, or just occasionally using a local bus or taxi. The routes will generally be roundtrip, though you can make an extended walk that will end up down the road or in another valley where there will be access to transportation back to your village. If you want, you can drive or take a bus a few miles to be able to start walking out of a different valley and see new horizons, returning to your village before nightfall.

2. **Backpacking.** Because villages and valleys are within walking distance of each other, the Lake District offers an unsurpassed chance to hike from valley to valley, sleeping in a different location every night. This is a somewhat more adventurous approach

to mountain walking—dearly loved by my husband—that we like to indulge in when we're in Cumbria. There are enough youth hostels, B&Bs, and country inns to allow you to backpack and have an overnight stay at whatever level of luxury you want. The advantage here is that you aren't limiting yourself to a roundtrip walk or return by the same route. You are able, in a few days, to move from region to region and enjoy vastly different scenery.

Seasons

You will find that almost any time of year presents a fine opportunity to visit the Lake District, though summer is clearly the busiest season. Expect changing weather whenever you come: on any given day it might rain, though you can spend a week there without any precipitation. But the climate on the whole—and the rain—tends to be mild. So as long as you come well-equipped you can enjoy your stay in most weather.

Spring in the Lake District presents the charms of that season. Flowers abound, including, of course, daffodils, which were immortalized in William Wordsworth's poem. The fresh green of new bracken brightens the landscape, followed by foxglove and other flowers. Summer is lush in an area frequently washed by showers and fall offers an autumnal air, the bracken golden and brown. The heather blooms over a long period. We have even walked in the Lake District in the middle of the winter. Well outfitted, ready for the cold as

WEATHER

"I am no novice in mountain mischiefs, but such a storm as this was I never witnessed, combining the intensity of the cold with the violence of the wind and rain. The rain-drops were pelted or, rather, slung against my face by the gusts, just like splinters of flint, and I felt as if every drop cut my flesh. . . . However I got safely over, and, immediately, all was calm and breathless, as if it was some mighty fountain just on the summit of Kirkstone, that shot forth its volcano of air, and precipitated huge streams of invisible lava down the road to Patterdale."

—Samuel Taylor Coleridge

we reached the crest of a mountain, we found it an extremely fine time for walking. Temperatures are much milder here than in the Alps or the Rockies, so the mountains can be enjoyed the entire year round—barring really serious storms.

Most important, whether you are a day-walker or a backpacker, *keep your clothing and other items in the rucksack well protected from possible rain.* You get wet on the way, but you'll be happy to have dry clothes to change into afterward. Good boots will get you through pretty much any weather and across numerous streams. Dried out overnight, they will be serviceable the next day.

Preparing for Backpacking

In the kind of walking that you'll be doing in the Lake District, there is little difference between day-walking and backpacking, aside from in the amount that you carry on your back. In either case you may do roughly the same amount of climbing and possibly hike about the same number of hours.

HINT:

Carry a plastic map case if you're in a district where you can expect rain. Fold the map to display the path you're taking. Keep the second map folded in behind. Even in the rain you can consult the map without having it disintegrate before your eyes.

You'll have to add a bit to your load, but you will find the difference in style exhilarating.

Let's say that you decide to make a four-day roundtrip, walking from A to B, sleeping at B the first night, from B to C, where you'll sleep the second night, from C to D, where you'll sleep the third night and then back to A on the fourth day. Ask your first hotel or B&B if you can leave your suitcase there for a few nights till you come back. Pack in everything that you would ordinarily take for a day's walk plus a change of underwear for the next three days, plus something decent (at least clean!) to change into in the evening. It can be the same thing every night—only your walking companions will have seen it before. Depending on what you wear in bed, you may need something for the night. You should try not to wear your hiking boots day and night, so carry either sneakers or sandals—what-

IF YOU DON'T WANT TO CARRY EXTRA WEIGHT:
If carrying is a problem, there are ways to avoid it in the Lake District. You can, for example, arrange for a taxi to pick up your bag from one hotel and deliver it to the next one. Then you can walk with just the usual weight on your back.

ever is light and comfortable. If you're staying in a hotel or B&B, you don't have to worry about carrying a towel and soap or bedding, so your pack should still be relatively light.

You should be able to get everything into the same daypack that you're using, provided that you cut down to the essentials, and then cut down more. Because daypacks vary in size, it's hard to know if your own pack will be big enough. But if you're walking with others, spread out some of the bulkier items, especially if some people have bigger packs. Don't overdo it: t-shirts can be worn more than once on a hike and pants too. But fresh socks and underwear, hairbrush, toothbrush, and toothpaste are important. You may want to bring a book. Needless to say, absolutely everything should be protected from possible rain, even if the weather forecast looks good.

In organizing a backpacking venture like this, it's best to make arrangements in advance, so that you can head straight for your hotel or hostel when you reach the village. A hot bath and a good dinner and you'll be fresh for the next day.

The experience of carrying with you everything that is utterly necessary for a day or two or for a week can be edifying. What are the essentials? What can you live without? When you boil it all down, it turns out that you need almost nothing, whether it's extra clothing, a hair dryer, toiletries or makeup, jewelry or more shoes. There's a feeling of great freedom knowing that whatever you need is there on your back. Try it!

Planning Your Walk

O.K. You're in the Lake District. You've given yourself a week for walking. You arrive at the train station in Windermere (or in Keswick by car, or wherever). Where do you go? How do you decide on your destinations and your routes? Let's start from square one and go through a short vacation in the Lake District and how you plan it.

Say that you want to stay put for a few days and then do a four-day backpacking ramble. The first days can then serve you as a warm-up, getting yourself fit for walking and comfortable in your surroundings. Choose your walks the way you would in the White Mountains or the Alps, increasing the number of hours walked and the height climbed every day to build up physical strength and stamina.

Now for the Backpacking!

Here's what you do, step by step.

- GET TWO KINDS OF MAPS: one that shows the whole region and is on a scale of something like one inch to one mile and the other that gives a specialized look at a particular section of the Lake District at a scale of two and a half inches to the mile (or 1:25,000). These are the Ordnance Survey maps mentioned in Chapter 4. The first map lets you make a large, general plan for the whole four-day itinerary. The second very detailed map is what you'll mainly use on the walk in order to note every farm you pass, every juncture of paths, in other words, every landmark. You should take both maps with you. In fact, if your path crosses into the territory of different maps (north-east, north-west, etc.) you may find that you will have to carry a few maps with you.

- READ THE LEGEND AT THE BOTTOM OF THE MAP. Make sure that you know, visually, the difference between the symbols for a path and a road. You want to avoid the latter. Walking on roads is harder on your feet and usually much more roundabout (not to mention having to watch out for cars). On one of my maps, paths are marked with a broken grey line, on another, a broken green line, so beware that colors can differ from map to map. On the detailed map you'll see an amazing array of notations: FB (footbridge), stepping stones across a stream (really!), hotels, farms, stiles.

- GET ALL THE INFORMATION THAT YOU CAN BEFORE PLOTTING YOUR ROUTE.

INFORMATION ON ROUTES AND DESTINATIONS:
- ✓ Check in at the Information Office that you'll find in most Lake District towns. They have all kinds of maps as well as knowledgeable people who can recommend routes. You can also contact them before you even arrive in Cumbria.
- ✓ Talk to people who have done walking in the Lake District.
- ✓ Get a book that outlines attractive walks. Check them out on your maps and see if you can piece together a longer route. Pay attention to what's said about distance, height, and difficulty.
- ✓ Talk to your innkeeper or the person who runs the bed and breakfast or Youth Hostel where you're staying.

With all this information open up the small-scale map on a table so that you can see the entire area at one glance.

- NOW YOU CAN WORK OUT A ROUTE. Your map will indicate height (the higher you go, the browner the color; the contours indicate it as well) so you can calculate how much climbing you'll have to do each day.

- CALCULATE THE LENGTH OF THE WALK using the string method or the wheeled measuring device described in Chapter 4. This will prevent total disasters, such as mapping out a fifteen-mile walk for one day instead of an eight-mile walk. Having made such miscalculations ourselves, I can assure you that dragging yourself into your B&B after eight o'clock at night when you'd expected to be there by six at the latest is no fun. (Especially, as happened with us, if they had your reservation down for the wrong Tuesday, but that's another story.)

Knowing all these facts, you can select your overnight goal for each day, combining the factors of distance, climbing and terrain. While the map indicates some hotels, there are plenty that are not shown. Check with the Visitor Center about hotels, B&Bs or hostels in the area and call ahead to reserve a place. Some books on Lake District walking also give information on accommodations.

Here's a Sample Four-Day Walking Plan:

Start out from Grasmere. This is a good center for walking—a charming village one of whose attractions is Dove Cottage where William Wordsworth and his family lived for many years in the first part of the nineteenth century. It is situated in a beautiful pastoral setting by the lake and with easy access to a number of picturesque mountain walks.

DAY 1. GRASMERE TO BORROWDALE.

Get an early start. There's not too much of a climb, but the distance is about ten miles. Take the path from Grasmere to Langdale. The village of Elterwater makes a good mid-morning stop: there's a fine tree shading a little village square as well as a good pub across the road. From Langdale pick up the Cumbria Way, a well-marked path that crosses the whole of Cumberland. The climb is about 1,500 feet to the pass and from the top the path follows the river, a long, graded descent. At the bottom you're in Borrowdale, one of the loveliest areas of the Lake District. There are hotels in a number of places. We tend to stay in Rothswaite, which is right on a stream and close to a number of trails.

DAY 2. BORROWDALE TO BUTTERMERE.

This is a shorter distance—about six miles—but with more climbing. The path crosses over Dale Head and then up Robinson, about a 2,000-foot climb. It's a wonderful walk that takes you up high to view a vast panorama of mountains and then drops you down toward Buttermere, a tiny settlement of farms and a couple of hotels and B&Bs located between two serene lakes. If you have a little extra energy before dinner, take one of the walks along the lakeside and enjoy the sunset. Both here and the previous night, you can have dinner either in one of the fine hotel dining rooms or in a local pub. Pubs serve good and varied food these days and in large quantities for hungry walkers (much cheaper than the more formal meal).

DAY 3. BUTTERMERE TO KESWICK.

Walk out of Buttermere along the northeast side of the lake (Buttermere) and then up onto the path that you followed from Dale Head the previous day, until you come to a left branch that takes you up Robinson and on toward Keswick. From Robinson you'll find yourself walking past farms and very bucolic Cumbrian scenery. Stay overnight anywhere in the Keswick area, either outside the town or in one of the hotels inside the town itself. It's a bustling place, filled with stores for locals as well as places for outfitting walking expeditions, a real center for the surrounding farm region.

DAY 4. KESWICK TO GRASMERE.

There are various ways to return to Grasmere. One that offers a fine walk would involve taking a bus from Keswick back to Rosthwaite. From there, follow the path along the stream behind the hotels and along a portion of the Cumbria Way to Stonethwaite. Then take a left branch of the path, eventually climbing up over a broad grassland ridge called Greenup Edge. At the top, if there's been a lot of rain, it may be boggy. Just pick your way over the spongy ground as best you can. Your boots are made for this. Follow the path down toward Grasmere Common and then into Grasmere. The walk is about eight or nine miles and includes a 2,000-foot climb, a good finish to four remarkable days of wandering.

In all of the places where you stop for the night you'll be able to put together food for your lunch break—pick up something in a local shop or ask your hotel to give you a packed lunch. In this way you can avoid having to carry enough food for four days, an additional and unnecessary weight. Remember to fill up your water bottles before leaving in the morning.

Look after your boots. You should always clean off your boots when you finish a walk. When they're dry, give them a good waxing to protect the leather and keep it water-resistant. If you're backpacking, take the tin of wax with you. This is especially important when walking in boggy or wet areas.

Backpacking in the Lake District

There's a difference between this kind of backpacking and the backpacking that you do out in the wilderness. What I've just described is easier, less risky and, though adventurous, less stressful.

If you plan a serious trek, you have to put much more thought and work into it before setting out. But this can give you a foretaste of what a full-scale backpacking expedition is like. Given that you would have to carry a much heavier load, that may never be an attractive option for you and you'll be happy to settle into the more manageable backpacking in an area like Cumbria—or in Switzerland or using the hut system of the White Mountains of New Hampshire or in California.

Walking with Your Family

If you're contemplating a trip with your family—or with a group of friends of diverse ages—consider the following points about the Lake District:

1. This is a fine area for families in that the initial altitude is low and the mountains themselves are not high. Lots of British families hike in the Lake District, as do school groups.
2. On the other hand, walking in Cumbria is definitely not as organized and clear-cut as walking in the Alps. Signposting can be minimal; paths are often rugged; there are few places for "pit

stops" along the way. You might walk for eight hours, from one valley to the next, and not find a restaurant or a lavatory.

3. The streams and tarns, gates, and stiles are all enjoyable for hiking children.

4. The weather—as in many mountain districts—isn't reliable. While that can be a nuisance, kids don't mind walking in the rain sometimes and may even relish it.

5. Members of the family who want to take a day off will enjoy strolling around Grasmere or Ambleside, Windermere or Keswick. All sorts of spots of historic or literary interest dot the area: the Wordsworth houses in Grasmere and Rydal, Ruskin's home, a beautiful garden connected with Peter Rabbit—yes, that's literature too. Bookshops are plentiful, packed with volumes on the history of Cumberland, hiking routes, poems of the Lake Poets and exciting illustrated works on mountain climbing. (Chris Bonnington, one of the world's most famous climbers, lives in Cumbria.) While there may not be a lot of theaters and concerts, the restaurants of the Lake District produce superb fresh trout, classic roast beef, and unbelievable cream desserts. After dinner, guests move into a separate room for their coffee and mints and often sit around, talking about the day's hiking and plans for the next day. After you've been there for a couple of days, you'll not only be asking for advice, but giving some too.

Trekking in the Himalayas

No, you don't have to read this chapter. It's about the way-out, the exotic. It's something you may have dreamed about, or something that comes up in your worst nightmares. But don't close the book: even in a chapter on trekking you'll find useful information for your own walking.

I started out hiking up the General Walsh trail at Bear Mountain, north of New York City, graduated to walking in the English Lake District and then to countless other places of immense scenic beauty. Only many years later did I begin to do treks in the Himalayas, both in Nepal and India, encountering an entirely new and incredible experience. So beware: this could happen to you if you're not careful.

Trekking can be done all over, on every continent. As you already know, there are long trails in the United States that can take weeks or months to traverse. Similar trails exist in South America and in Europe too. In Switzerland, for example, various trail systems for long-distance hikers thread their way through the Alps. The possibilities are endless. After many, many years—decades—of walking in the mountains of Europe and North America, we decided to look further afield and chose the Himalayas for extended treks.

Why the Himalayas?

Why did we choose such a distant—and different—area for our trekking?

1. The mountains there are incredibly high. You find yourself in an area where the mountains tower at 20,000 feet and higher.
2. The area is vast. You feel that you could go on forever in this region with mountain ranges stretching away, one beyond the other, endlessly. The effect is overwhelming.

3. The region of the Himalayas is exotic. On the trek the hiker finds herself in scenery—forests with rich undergrowth and hanging plants, remote villages, superb mountain panoramas, wildlife of a different kind (monkeys, for example)—that is far from anything she has experienced in hikes closer to home.

4. Encounters with people here are unique. With a culture so different and with lives lived so cut off from towns, people offer a friendly and curious welcome to strangers. We have found ourselves—after a week literally without seeing another person—entering a village where all the villagers await our approach, hands together in a position of prayer, greeting us with a shy "Nemaste" as we approach: the first outsiders they have seen in months.

5. This is a way to get very close to nature: walking on paths used by local villagers and herds, sleeping in tents or tiny teahouses, waking to the rising sun.

6. Trekking involves something that no one can replicate without doing it by foot themselves. The paths are far beyond the reach of any vehicle. We have followed trails that were a good week's walk from the nearest road, even a dirt road.

7. You can be really cut off when you're trekking in the Himalayas. This may be an attraction or a turn-off. But on a walk of this kind, you won't be picking up news on a radio. The world outside the mountains simply doesn't exist.

8. If you don't want to work out your own arrangements, there are excellent companies that organize treks very professionally. Airfare aside, you can put together a trek complete with porters and a sherpa for a reasonable price. So while this is an exotic trip you don't have to feel that you are taking risks or spending a fortune.

9. Although it may be hard work, you'll have a feeling of accomplishment at the end

> *"Hills whose heads touch heaven."*
> —Othello, *William Shakespeare*

of your trek like none you've ever known. And a host of memories to last a lifetime—or until the next trek.

The Nature of Trekking

Trekking does not equal the sum of ten or twenty day-walks, one after another, on an ordinary hiking vacation. There is a cumulative effect that has to be considered. On a trek you are gaining ground—and altitude—without returning to home base every night. By the time you've walked three or four days you are probably above the 10,000-foot mark and still advancing. You're not coming back to a hot bath or the comforts of a bed every evening. If a problem arises, you have to deal with it—or live with it—till you finish your trek. It's also a much more intensive social experience, affecting your interaction with the people you're walking with. All of these factors contribute to a qualitatively different experience. In some ways it is, naturally, more difficult. In other ways it is more rewarding.

RELATIVITY:

You have to pinch yourself to believe the height of the mountains that you're looking at. By the time you get to 8,000 feet on a trek, the 25,000-foot mountain that you're looking at doesn't seem so high, more like looking at the Matterhorn in Zermatt. It's all relative.

Preparing for a Trek

You can be far more casual about getting ready for a day-walk than preparing for a trek. Because of the extended effort made, your body has to be in very fit condition. Everything said in Chapter 3 should be magnified. You want to make sure that you're at as good a weight as you can manage, although there's little doubt that you'll take off pounds in the course of the trek. But start well.

You'll have to build up your stamina as far as possible. This includes concentrating on walking up and down to the maximum. Before one of our treks, we used a set of steps leading from one level of town to another—there were over a hundred of them—and walked up and down them countless times day after day.

Yes, work out at the gym regularly—on the treadmill, on the steps, cycling—if that's your favorite form of exercise. Because you don't necessarily have the same amount of flexibility on a trek as you do when planning a day-walk, your body has to be in the best possible tone and strength. On a day-walk you can turn around in the middle and go back, or slow your pace. On a trek, you are usually aiming for a specific place for your overnight stop and will have no choice but to keep going until you get there. Once in Nepal we had to take shelter for quite a while during an unexpected and very heavy rainstorm. By the time we got started again we realized that we still had a long way to go. In the end, we straggled into the campsite as it was getting dark. While some days can be only three or four hours, you will find that others will stretch out to seven, eight, or even more.

Nothing will make your trek more successful than plenty of exercise beforehand.

Planning Your Trek

A trek has to be minutely organized. By now a great number of books are available that deal with the art of trekking or backpacking. *Read up on trekking in the area.* Besides the general books, many concentrate on a specific trail or area. Before our first Himalayan trek we got hold of every book on Himalayan trekking that we could put our hands on, trying to absorb the essential facts about what we hoped to do.

In the course of our reading, we realized that there are two basic ways to walk in the Himalayas: sleeping in teahouses along the way or camping out. And there were two different kinds of areas: those with teahouses and those without. The second type of area offered what was called wilderness trekking, away, as the authors put it, from the "toilet-paper trail." (Actually from our experience later, the trails are kept pretty clean.) After reading a couple of books we could see clearly that we were not going to want the crowds, the signs of "civilization," the teahouse type of hiking. So we opted for a wilderness trail.

This is a major decision because once you decide on wilderness walking you have to carry a tent, sleeping bag, food, all the paraphernalia. Few people do this kind of tour carrying everything on their own back. It's too much of a strain, given the terrain and the altitude. Porters can be hired inexpensively and this is what most Himalayan walkers do, even many who do the teahouse routes.

Teahouses

People planning a trek on their own, with or without the help of a porter, find this the least complicated option. It is also the thriftiest way to trek in the Himalayas. The cost of a night in a teahouse is negligible. The walking itself is no harder or easier, but at least you don't have to carry much food and can always find a place to sleep and eat and maybe even shower. Specific trails in Nepal, for example, such as in Langtang or in the Annapurna region are dotted with occasional tiny buildings which cater to the heavier demand of the popular treks. Some routes get overloaded with trekkers; when planning, try to avoid them if this isn't what you're looking for.

The accommodations in many of the teahouses are clean and pleasant, if basic. Freshly cooked local food is available. Even if you've been walking alone all day, there is the pleasure of camaraderie in the late afternoons, meeting other trekkers from all over the world. The atmosphere is convivial.

Wilderness Trekking

Although with this option there are few or no teahouses there are certainly real—and very clear—paths. These paths were not created for trekkers, although trekkers use them. They provide the only way of communicating between villages high up in the Himalayas. Some of them are Hindu or Buddhist pilgrim routes to holy shrines or lakes. It is not uncommon to find countless stone steps progressing up a steep mountainside. On these paths you can have interesting encounters with local people. One day, making our way from one place to another, we found a man walking behind us, carrying some woven mats on his back. When we stepped aside to let him pass, he indicated that he would continue to follow—he just wanted the company for a while. It turned out that he was carrying the mats on what would be a three-day walk so that he could sell them in a larger village. With the money he would buy a sack of salt and carry it home. A week to buy a sack of salt!

Walking in these areas you feel that the wheel hasn't yet been invented. There are literally no wheeled vehicles. The main means of transportation is by foot; the main way of moving goods is on your back. In a way, a trekker in these parts feels that she has not only come to a very remote geographical area; she has also gone back in time, not hundreds but thousands of years.

Organizing a Trek

There are plenty of tour companies that take groups trekking in the Himalayas. You can join a ready-made group or have a company put together the whole trek for you and your friends: sardar (to lead the group), porters, cook, sherpas, and food supplies. Some of the companies are in America or England; others are in Nepal or India.

When we first thought about doing a trek, we assumed that we would join a group organized by a very fine tour arranger in London. The more I thought about it the more concerned I was. Who would be the people in the group? What was their level of mountain skills? Would we be compatible? What if they were a bunch of stragglers who dragged along and slowed the rest of the group down? Worse still, what if they were all tall, muscular guys who ran up mountains for fun? What if we kept them back and earned their unmitigated disdain? After a lot of thought we decided on two things:

1. We definitely wanted one of the less popular, more unspoiled treks where there'd be few people.
2. We would make up a group of just the two of us and have the company organize a specialized trek for us alone. Although it seems like a very luxurious thing to do, we discovered that it would not cost much more than participating in a larger group. Being alone, we had an unforgettable opportunity to interact with the sardar and sherpas and get to see local life personally to the maximum.

Our taste doesn't have to be yours. There are great advantages in going in groups, including the social factor of interacting with a lot of (hopefully) like-minded people. On one trek—on a teahouse route—we became friendly with a number of people in various groups and would meet up with them in the evening, just for a chat. Our daughter Rachel joined an English group trekking in Karakoram in Pakistan, people of all ages and types, and they had a terrific time—an unforgettable time—together.

Look for advertisements, consult a good travel agent or check the Internet. Make sure you're getting a reliable company that will look after you well. We use a local trekking company that organizes climbs up Mount Everest. While our treks are very tame compared to that we still want a highly responsible group whom we can count on in case of emergencies—and we have had a few. We also want food that will be safe to eat and water that can be drunk without worry of stomach upsets. A good company will make sure that this is what you get.

One Day in the Life of a Trekker

This is a description of an organized trek, if it's well done. Trekkers get up early. They want a good start to the day and the campsite has to be cleared before going on.

- **Wake-up call.** The day starts at 6 A.M. with the sound of your tent zipper being pulled up slightly. The cookboy calls out "Morning! Water!" Two basins of warm water have been placed just outside the tent. Get up and get washed. That's what the water's there for. Did you pack a mirror in your backpack? We bring one for my husband, who likes to shave, even on a trek. Me? I try not to look in a mirror till I'm off the trek. A pleasure!
- **Breakfast.** A good breakfast is important. You need a lot of energy—calories, carbohydrates—to keep you going. Take your choice: eggs, oatmeal, baked beans, toast—maybe all of them. You'd be surprised how much food you can put away on a trek. (And not gain weight.)
- **Pack up and leave.** By seven, breakfast is over, tents taken down and packed, and the site left as it was when you arrived.

STAFF ON AN ORGANIZED TREK:

Sardar. *He's the leader of the expedition. He usually knows the area well, makes decisions on the route and is generally responsible for the safety of the trekkers. He can speak English. The others may, but not necessarily.*

Sherpas. *These men are mountain experts and assist the sardar. Many of them come from the Everest area and are accustomed to high altitude living. They help trekkers in any difficult situation and make sure that no one in the group goes astray. The sherpas are responsible for setting up the campsite and dismantling it. They tend to be young and most hope to attain the level of sardar someday.*

Cook. *He's the man who makes you feel that life is almost luxurious, even in trying conditions. From morning till night he supplies delicious and varied food. He tends to stay by the cook tent and is mainly in the company of the staff.*

Cookboy. *If there is one on the trek, this is a young man who may have been a porter until recently and is aiming to be a cook with time. He's the one who will bring you your hot water for washing in the morning, set up the table for dinner, serve meals, and generally be an aid to the cook.*

Porters. *These men, of all ages, carry incredibly heavy loads—tents, sleeping bags, kitchen utensils, all bound together in big clusters—on their backs, aided by a strap across the forehead. They tend to keep to themselves, speak no foreign language and run on ahead, barefoot, leaving the trekkers to follow. (The better trekking companies make sure that they have reliable footwear for high altitudes and don't carry absurd weights.) There are also women porters, who carry heavy loads and assist on treks. Some women specifically request women porters for their trek.*

Your trek may offer more or less than this. But the description here is typical.

Organized treks provide toilet facilities, usually a small tent covering a hole dug in the ground. A roll of toilet paper may be stuck in there. Next to the hole is a pile of the earth that was removed. The technique is squat and kick, just enough earth to cover over what's in the hole and ready for the next user. When you break up camp, the hole is completely filled in. (On our most recent trek we had the luxury of all luxuries: a toilet seat mounted on wire legs that was placed directly over the hole, so you could sit instead of squatting. It's light and folds up easily for transporting. We were understandably gratified to have it!)

- **Walk!** Now the day's trekking has begun. Decisions about where the group stops for lunch or for the night are usually made by the cook, or the cook in conjunction with the sardar. He has to find a place where he can set up his kitchen and find a source of water. Lunch is usually pretty early in the day. As you last ate a little after 6 A.M., you'll be happy to dig into lunch at 10:30 or 11. (That's when the porters eat their first meal.) We usually get a hot lunch, though sometimes a group will be served cold food. In India on a trek we were given a tiffin box every day, with compartments inside filled with sandwiches, fresh fruit, dried fruit, and a little treat for dessert. But in Nepal we tend to have a cooked lunch, lighter than dinner, but with plenty of carbohydrates: french fries, baked beans. There's also tea or coffee. What you drink most is water. The water has been boiled and filtered by the cook and is given to you, still hot, at night. By the morning it's cool. Because of the hot water, it's usually recommended to bring metal water bottles. They make great "hot water bottles" on very cold nights.

- **Continue trekking.** In the course of the day you will find yourself in the most amazing scenery. Perhaps your walk will take you through forests rich in rhododendron or bamboo. Or balancing on the edge of terraced fields of bright green millet, walking mile after mile. Or climbing up a rocky path, passing herds of cattle and yaks making their way down for the winter.

The scenery will present endless delightful variations and one thing is certain: nothing about the trek will be boring.

- **Arriving at your destination for the night**. The day's trekking can finish at any time from 2 P.M. to 6 P.M., varying from day to day. The length of the day's walk is a function of the route and your speed. Unlike many other areas, trekking in the Himalayas involves a lot of climbs and descents in a given day. While the altitude change from start to finish may be only 2,000 feet, you may have climbed a total of 3,000–4,000 feet, with all the ups and downs. There are some terrains where you simply cannot limit the distance walked, because it will be impossible to find an acceptable intermediate campsite.

- **Tea.** Now is the time to take off your boots and put on sport shoes or slippers. Whatever else you bring on the trek, don't forget to pack sneakers. You need something comfortable to change into at the end of a long day's walk. (And if anything goes wrong with your boots, they can act as an inferior "spare.") It's also a good idea to bring along a light pair of sandals or slippers for the evening. If you have to get up in the middle of the night and make your way to the toilet tent you're not going to want to start maneuvering your feet into heavy boots.

The cook will have set up his kitchen in his own tent; water will be boiling and cooking preparations made. You can sit back on a little camp chair, have a cup of tea and some cookies or peanut butter and crackers and pull out a book. Or play cards or chess. Or take a walk around your campsite, see the views, take photographs. Perhaps there's a village down the path that you'd like to see. This is a good opportunity, while the sky is still light, to write in your diary.

It's also the time for bathing. Once again you'll be given a bowl of hot water for washing. It's terrifically important that you use it every day: get undressed (at least one part at a time), no matter how cold it is and wash yourself thoroughly, with soap. There's hell to pay if you don't change your underclothes and keep clean. This is a cardinal rule if you're doing long-time walking. If there's a group around and you need privacy, either use the front section of your tent, where there's no floor, or take over the toilet tent for a short time and wash in there. It takes a little practice to avoid getting yourself dirty again after you've washed and before you've got your feet into clean socks, but it can be done. We were lucky on the most recent trek to have an actual shower tent brought along and that was heavenly, as it came with a portable shower that the cook filled with warm water. But perhaps that's too much to dream of!

Cleanliness is even more important if you are menstruating. Whenever you go out on a walk of more than one day—not just on a trek—make sure that you bring along a small package with a few tampons or sanitary napkins, plus a plastic bag for carrying out used ones for disposal at the end of the day's walk.

VERY IMPORTANT:
No matter what the weather or inconvenience, wash every day. Cleanliness is a key to wellness on a trek.

Because of additional exercise or other changes, your period can surprise you at an odd time. That is almost predictable! No matter how you handle the bathing problem—standing on one foot near a bowl of water, using a shower, washing one area of your body at a time—you must keep yourself clean. For feminine hygiene, one easy method is to bring along pre-moistened towelettes, such as the kind used for wiping babies' bot-

Bring along at least two towels. They get dirty and musty easily and are often hard to dry out on a trek. Keep one especially for your face and hands.

toms. It may not be as effective as real soap-and-water washing, but will certainly serve the purpose. I don't recommend it, though, as your only method of washing.

- **Dinner.** There is usually a special dining tent for trekkers to eat in. Dinner is a serious meal, starting with soup and followed by a variety of concoctions some of which will be Indian or Nepali, but might also be Chinese or European-style. The cook can make a four-star meal out of the basic ingredients carried by the porters. Sometimes he will buy some fresh vegetables from villagers along the way. What he can put together from his supplies, cooked over gas fires set up on the ground is remarkable. We've even been served fresh apple pie, baked over a campfire. After my first trek, I more or less suffered from separation anxiety at losing our cook!

- **Time to sleep.** Once it's dark and dinner is over, most people don't sit around very long. They're tired. It's cold. They've finished a long day of solid walking and look forward to another one tomorrow. And they have to get up at six in the morning. So by nine P.M.—a little earlier or later—trekkers get ready to get into their sleeping bags and hunker down for the night. When it's really cold, we use two sleeping bags, one inside the other, for extra warmth. (Either bring a pillow, or at least a pillow case that you can stuff towels and other soft things into.) People sleep soundly after such an active day. The exception is at higher altitudes—above 10,000 feet or even lower—when your sleep may be hampered by restlessness or vivid dreams.

Possible Problems on a Trek

Many of the same problems that may afflict ordinary day-walking can occur during a trek. But because of the nature of a trek, these problems may take on a greater dimension or risk. Knowing how to handle potential problems is essential for the hiker. Let's go over a few of them:

High Altitude

If you are walking in a high-altitude area, you should know how to deal with height, even if you come back to your hotel every night. By high altitude, I mean 10,000 feet and above, though even at lower heights people can be affected. Travellers who fly into Mexico City often notice that their body behaves somewhat differently during the first day or two. You may find yourself a little breathless just climbing a flight of stairs.

It is much easier to deal with high altitude if you reach it by walking than by flying in or driving up in a day. *Indeed, the key to acclimatizing to height is to attain it gradually.* On a trek, the starting point might be at 4,000–5,000 feet and it could be a few days before you reach high altitude. This is ideal for conditioning yourself for the greater height that is ahead.

What are the effects of height on a hiker? You can find yourself working harder to do something that causes no problem at sea level. Even bending over to tie a shoelace at 12,000 feet can be a bit of an effort. That's normal. The point is not to push yourself beyond your comfort level. Walk a little more slowly. Don't expect to make it up a mountain as quickly. *Ideally, if you're on a trek, the rule of thumb is not to sleep higher than 1,000 feet above where you slept the night before when you reach an altitude of 9,000–10,000 feet.* This means that if you're aiming at a campsite at 15,000 feet, it should take you five days to reach it from your initial campsite at 10,000.

In terms of day-walking, keep in mind that if you are staying in a center that is extremely high to begin with—Aspen, for example—by the time you've climbed two or three thousand feet, you're at the kind of height where your walking can be affected. Some people feel the effects of height at even 8,000–9,000 feet. Take it easy and don't attempt too much the first few days.

Altitude Sickness

Beyond the ordinary discomforts encountered walking at high altitudes, there are also clinically recognizable symptoms that require quick and serious attention. Acute Mountain Sickness can be life-threatening. Persistent problems caused by high altitude—severe headache, loss of appetite, nausea, dizziness, apathy—indicate a situation that requires immediate care. The most effective and time-honored treatment is to take the sufferer to a lower altitude, right away, even if she has to be carried. In most cases once the person descends some way down, the symptoms will begin to disappear.

Mountain sickness can affect even the healthiest people, in peak condition. Climbers can be afflicted by it as well as skiers. Remain aware of the symptoms and alert to any worsening condition.

Cold

Once you've climbed a few thousand feet you'll start feeling the cold, not so much when you're walking as when you are at rest. After arriving at your campsite—and certainly after washing—you'll want to put on lots more clothing, much more than you ever take for a day-hike. An anorak won't be enough: you need a good warm jacket. And lots of layers underneath. It's now, while you're sitting around by the tent, having dinner and later getting into your sleeping bag, that you'll need to protect yourself against the cold. At such a time, there's nothing as good as thermal underwear. It's much too warm to wear during the day while walking, but terrific in the evening. Remember that long-sleeved and long-legged silk long underwear mentioned in Chapter 5? It's excellent on a trek. It keeps the heat in. Do you need it? Yes. Up at 14,000 feet, you'll be wearing a woolen cap and gloves at dinner!

Hypothermia

This is another, much more severe, problem related to altitude and cold, though it can affect people at lower heights as well. Hypothermia, in the extreme—the inability of the body to retain its heat—can also lead to death.

It is important, when hiking in cold weather, to wear sufficient clothing and to eat enough to keep your body working. Although it is true that the body keeps warm while climbing, there is a point of diminishing returns if a person is insufficiently dressed, clothing is wet, or the walker has slowed down or stopped.

Once someone is suffering from hypothermia, get her into warm, dry clothing and keep her awake and moving, ideally toward some shelter. This is where all the warm and waterproof clothing you've been carrying on your back prove their worth. Never leave a person who seems to be suffering from hypothermia—shivering, unable to keep up, mentally confused—alone or untended. Eventually, such a person will become drowsy and lose consciousness. This can mark the beginning of the end.

Unexpected Weather

Nothing is more changeable or unexpected than weather in the mountains. For this reason your backpack must contain anything that you might need in case of an emergency, inclement weather, or hunger. On your back, if you planned well, you are carrying a small multipurpose wardrobe, a well-chosen pharmacy, and emergency rations. They are to help you avoid any potentially dangerous situation. If you are on an organized trek, your duffel bag is carried by a porter and that holds all of your clothing for the trek, extra shoes, toilet paper, reading matter, and anything else you want on the trek. In your backpack, which is quite light, you will be carrying rain gear, water, first-aid supplies, a sweater, and—if you're in the Himalayas—an umbrella. Ready for anything!

> *"Now the last word lies with the God of weathers and to confide in Him is the duty of every sincere sportsman."*
> —Baron Ehrenfried Gunther von Huenefeld, 1928

Unexpected Changes

Anything can happen on a trek and it often does. On one trek, we discovered that two river crossings where we'd expected a bridge, had to be made by fording. On that same trek, because one path had disappeared, the new one had a patch that was incredibly narrow and with a sheer 1,000-foot drop to our right. On another trek heavy and unexpected rains had caused massive landslides. Our path was washed out and other ways out of the area had to be found—and this happened during the "dry season" (the third week in October). In each case, because we had a first-rate team, we managed everything in relative safety. On other treks, the weather was perfect, the trail offered no unpleasant surprises and everything went as we had planned. Being in good physical shape, though, is a must in case things go wrong.

Illness

It can happen anywhere: you pick up some bug, run a fever, have an upset stomach. At home these are minor occurrences, soon forgotten. On a trek, you have to find a way to deal with it. Ordinarily, if you find that you are not in a state to continue, there is enough elasticity in the schedule to allow you to have a rest day and get over whatever it is. In terms of stomach upset, your cook will help out. I was once given a bowl of garlic soup that was not only delicious but impressively effective—

a local Nepali remedy that the cook prepared. The sardar carries various medications for problems that might affect his clients. We usually bring with us a broad spectrum antibiotic and anti-diarrhea pills (neither of which we have ever used). If a trekker becomes too ill to go on, or breaks a leg, for example, the sherpas will carry her out. In extreme situations, a sherpa will run to the nearest village that has a phone—and they can make incredible time when they're on their own—and get additional help, even a helicopter. (I don't have any personal stories on this variation!)

The Pill
There's been a fair amount written about the possible danger of women on oral contraceptives walking at high altitude for extended periods of time. So far, however, there is no good statistical evidence that taking them significantly increases your chance of a blood clot. To play it safe, if you find yourself walking at extremely high altitude (over 16,000 feet) for a few weeks—and this will affect very few women—you might want to stop taking the pill, according to your doctor's advice. One dangerous combination should be mentioned: the pill plus high altitude plus smoking. This should definitely be avoided. If you cannot stop the smoking, then stop taking the pill.

All of this advice pertains as well to women taking hormone replacement.

Summing Up
You may find a trek an enchanting experience and when you finish one, you may immediately start dreaming about the next one. There is no question that a trek—whether in the Himalayas or the Andes, the Sierra Nevadas or Appalachians—is uniquely different from anything you would ordinarily do in your life. So you may find yourself, in the long run, enjoying mountain vacations of the usual kind at times and at others, heading off for the exotic, the more challenging and the unusual.

You may find that the idea of a long-distance walk over a period of days, weeks, or months is not at all your cup of tea. That will in no way detract from the fun that you can get from the mountains. Nothing will match the excitement, whether it's the start of a day-long or month-long walk, of stepping out fresh on a new trail, checking your path, adjusting your backpack and heading up.

Index

Cardigan (mountain), 138–39, 140
cardiovascular fitness, 28, 29, 30
Catskills, 149
cellular phone, 74
children, 85–89; babysitters, 124;
    teenagers, 89–93; using an
    altimeter, 48; young, 85–89
climatic zones, 98
clothing, 49–61; for backpacking,
    161–62; take on hike, 63–65
col, 39, 63, 116–17
compass, 41–47; children, 91;
    importance of, 153; pack in, 71
Continental Divide Trail, 146, 147
contours, 39, 40
contrasts between U.S. and Europe,
    130–35
coordinates, 40
crampons, 34, 93; boots for, 51; on
    snow, 148
Cumbria Way, 164

day pack. See backpack
DEET, 134. See also insect repellent
dehydration, 89
descent. See downhill walking
diet, 31–32
doctor, 28
dogs, 94
downhill walking, 26, 120; timing,
    18, 122
drinking water, 60, 69

Edelweiss, 109
Eiger, 13
endorphins, 32
English tourists, 21, 101–2,
    112–13

etiquette: food, 106–7; garbage, 141;
    greeting hikers, 133; passing on
    narrow path, 119
exercise, 15–32; preparing for trek,
    172–73

family, 77–95; walking in the Lake
    District, 166–67
feet, 66, 108–9, 125
Findeln, 113, 114
fitness: importance of, 29, 183;
    psychology of, 32. See also
    exercise
flowers, 90; alpine, 98, 115, 117, 121;
    in Himalayas, 170; in Lake
    District, 153–54, 159
Furi, 105, 115

glaciers, 93, 115, 121; Mount
    Rainier, 147; in Zermatt area,
    110
Gornergrat, 56, 112–13, 121–22
GPS, 73
grading walks, 19–21
Grand Canyon, 55, 147–48
grandparents, 85
Grand Teton National Park, 152
Grasmere, 65, 153, 167;
    backpacking, 164–65
Green Mountains, 129, 149
Grindelwald, 13
Grünsee, 113, 121
guidebook, 136, 137
guides, 93

hats, 58, 64
high altitude sickness, 180–81; in
    children, 84

New Hampshire, 134–35; rain, 65

Wellenkuppe, 110, 111

Wengen, 98

White Mountains, 127–30, 138–41, 149

wild animals, 87; in the Himalayas, 170; in the Lake District, 157; in Switzerland, 115, 117, 119, 120; in the United States 143, 146, 149, 151–52

Windermere, 158, 167

Zermatt, 15, 56, 98–126; guides office, 122, 124; with kids, 91–92; Tourist Information Office, 101, 124

Zinal Rothorn, 110, 111

Z'mutt, 104–7, 115